Class Piano Resource Materials

Level Two

(Fifth Edition)

Compiled and edited by
W. Daniel Landes

Class Piano Resource Materials
Level Two
(Fifth Edition)

Other Class Piano Resource Materials are available from Smith Creek Music, PO Box 140446, Nashville, TN 37214
Please e-mail us at info@smithcreekmusic.com or visit our WEB site at www.smithcreekmusic.com for ordering information.

Introduction

These Class Piano Resource Materials were compiled for use in the secondary piano program at Belmont University, Nashville, TN. Consequently, the content has been shaped to a large extent by the various degree programs at that school and in particular, the Piano Proficiency Examination. Every school/department of music has some type of piano proficiency evaluation that music majors must past in order to complete their degree requirements. The various parts of the proficiency examination are the basic piano skills: repertory, scales and arpeggios, chords, harmonizing melodies, improvisation, transposition, etc. Consequently, the Class Piano Resource Materials are designed to prepare the student to pass a piano proficiency examination. Although intended for use in college classes, the materials are broad enough to be used in any class piano setting where there is a need for a graded series of books with a broad range of musical styles.

SCOPE OF THE MATERIALS

The Class Piano Resource Materials are arranged in five books by level of difficulty: Preparatory Level (no prior keyboard experience is assumed), Level One, Level Two, Level Three, and Level Four. Each level is organized according to specific goals that are spelled out clearly at the beginning of the book. Theory skills are not addressed in great detail because it is assumed that secondary piano classes are required in conjunction with the various theory classes such as Fundamentals of Music, Diatonic Harmony, etc. Detailed pedagogical information is outside the scope of these Resource Materials because it is believed that the instructor will give the necessary explanation of keyboard technique, theory, etc. Nevertheless, all the books in the various levels are organized in a more or less increasing level of difficulty if the instructor chooses to use them in that way. In addition, a suggested assignment schedule based on a 15-week semester is included in each level to aid the instructor in preparing weekly lesson plans.

DESCRIPTION OF THE MATERIALS

In selecting the materials, specific composers and periods of music were a strong factor. Each level contains representative repertory by classical composers such as Bach and Beethoven. Twentieth century classical music composers such as Bartók, Persichetti, and Schoenberg are included as well as representative pieces in various styles composed specifically for these books by the author and colleagues. Each level includes music in a popular style. These are not arrangements of popular tunes but are original compositions which appear here for the first time. It is hoped that the choice of repertory and other material will give the student a well-rounded musical experience and help develop keyboard and musicianship skills necessary for the professional musician.

INTEGRATION OF TECHNOLOGY

Each level (book) has an accompanying interactive computer application that been designed as an addition resource, including links to a WEB site. The application runs on Apple Macintosh computers using system OSX 10.2 and higher. Versions for Windows computers, IPads, etc. may be available in the future. Detailed information regarding the implementation of the computer software is available on the website:

www.smithcreekmusic.com

COPYRIGHTS

Every effort was made to contact the owners of copyrights for permission to make settings or use pieces. If mistakes have occurred, they will be corrected as soon as possible. Please email us at:

info@smithcreekmusic.com.

The author is grateful to the owners of copyrighted material who have granted permission to use their works. Where copyrighted material is used, a copyright notice appears at the bottom of the page.

Table of Contents

APPENDIXES

For more resources, please visit the WEB SITE at:

www.smithcreekmusic.com

General Goals
(Level Two)

1. Reinforce orientation to the keyboard:

   -- demonstrate an understanding of proper sitting position and hand position
   -- play in the correct octave
   -- demonstrate an understanding of basic hand positions: 5-finger hand positions, octave hand positions

2. Play major and harmonic minor scales in Group I; play major, natural, harmonic, and melodic minor scales in Group II. (see explanation in the scale section of this volume).

3. Play assigned repertory pieces with acceptable proficiency.

4. Demonstrate an understanding of the proper use of the sustain pedal.

5. Play root position major and minor triads on any note.

6. Play block-style cadences in major and minor keys through two accidentals.

7. Harmonize simple melodies using primary chords and some secondary dominants.

8. Improvise simple melodies (chord tones, passing tones, neighbor tones) over given chord progressions in major and minor keys through two accidentals.

9. Create simple improvised arrangements of familiar melodies.

10. Transpose a single line (treble or bass clef) of simple pieces up and down a half step and whole step.

11. Establish major and minor keys on the white notes of the piano by playing the chord progression of Cadence #1 (see explanation in the Cadence section of this volume).

12. Continue to develop concepts of sight reading.

13. Play simple technical exercises.

14. Continue to develop concepts of style and musicianship and demonstrate these in the performance of assigned repertory:

   -- expression
   -- articulation
   -- dynamics
   -- tempo

Class Notes

German Dance

What Wondrous Love Is This?

Playing Soldiers

*Play the G in the LH staccato so the RH G will sound.

Soldier's March

Burleske

Sunrise

From *For Children, Book I*, No. 1. Sunrise, 1909

Duo

a tempo
22
p
3
2
2
3
2
4 5 3 1
1
25
3 5 2
5
4
1
5
28
a tempo
3 5
poco rit.
1
5
4
1
f
2
2
3
31
3 4
1 3 2 1
4 1
4 1
5
2
1
4
33
4
3
molto rit.
3
4

Prologue

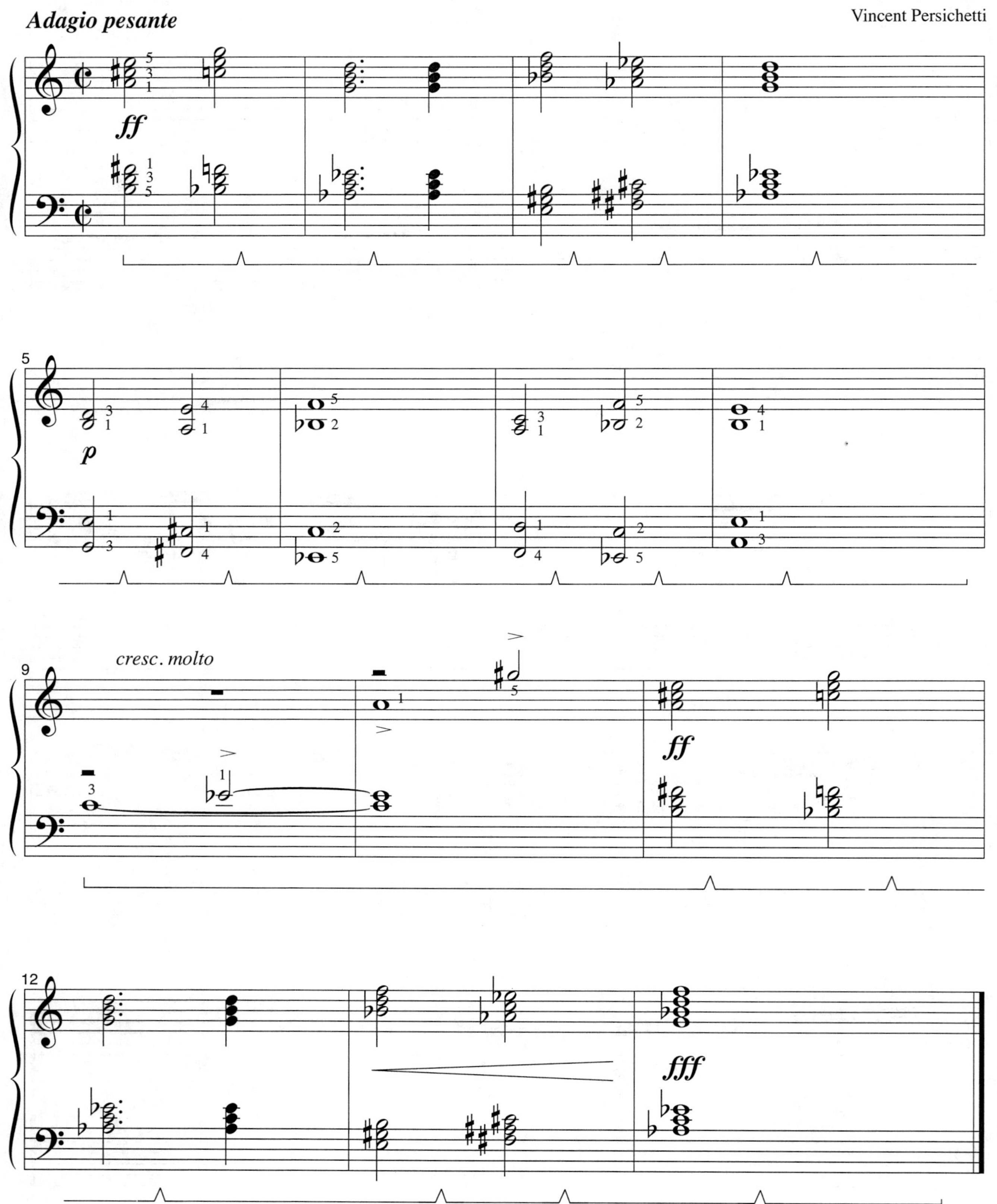

Exhortation

Allegro

From *Wyeth's Repository of Sacred Music,*
Part 2nd, 1820.
Adapted and arr. by WDL

Minuet in G

Allegretto

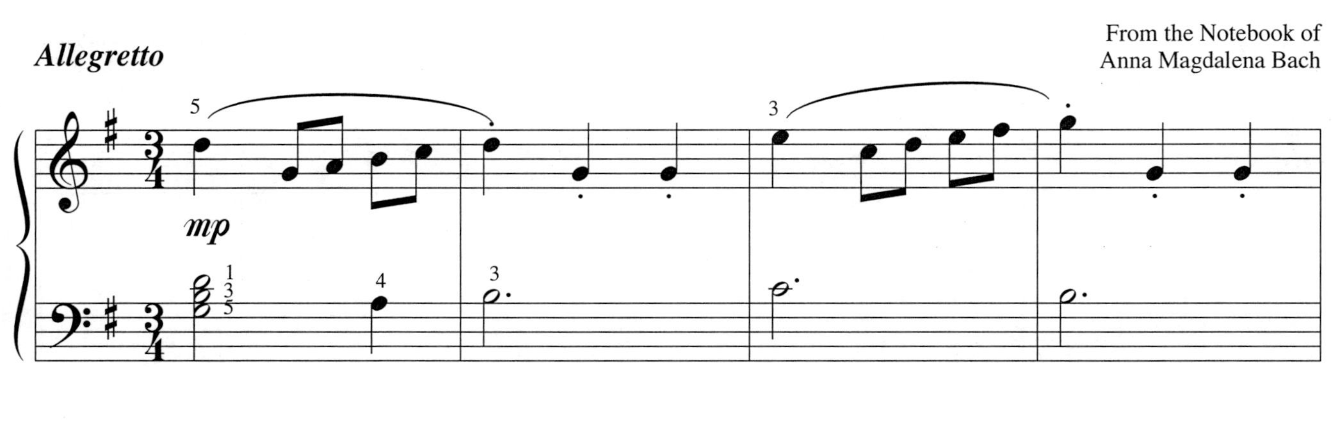

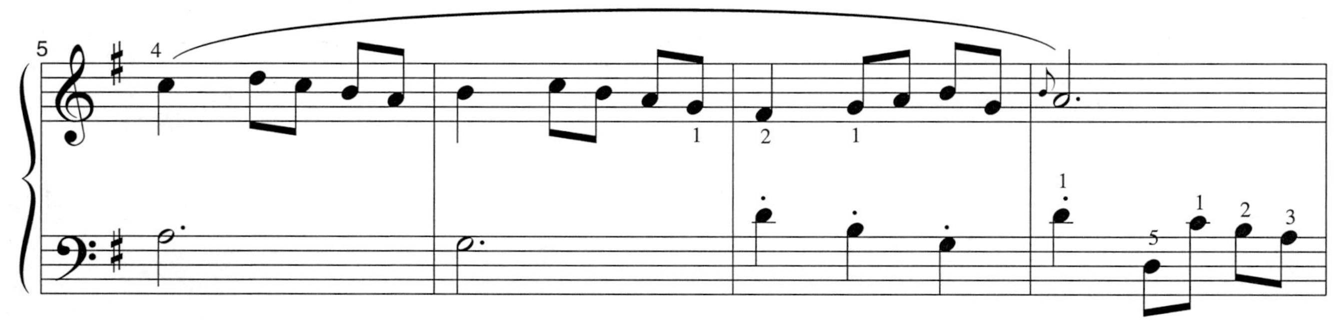

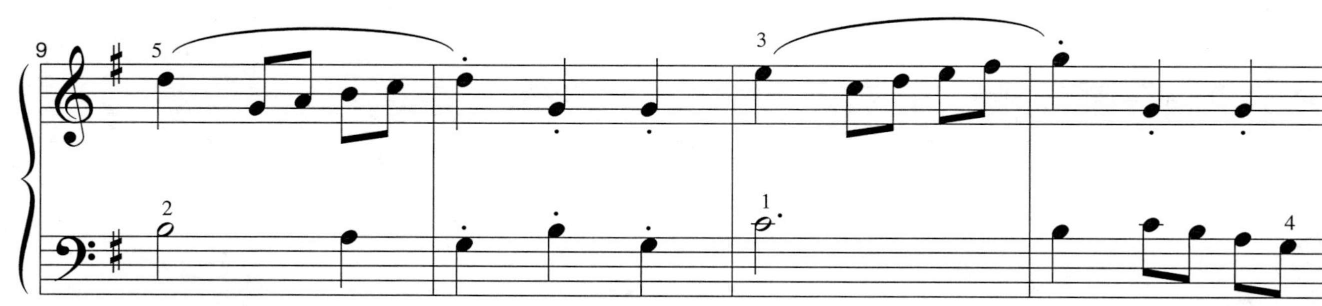

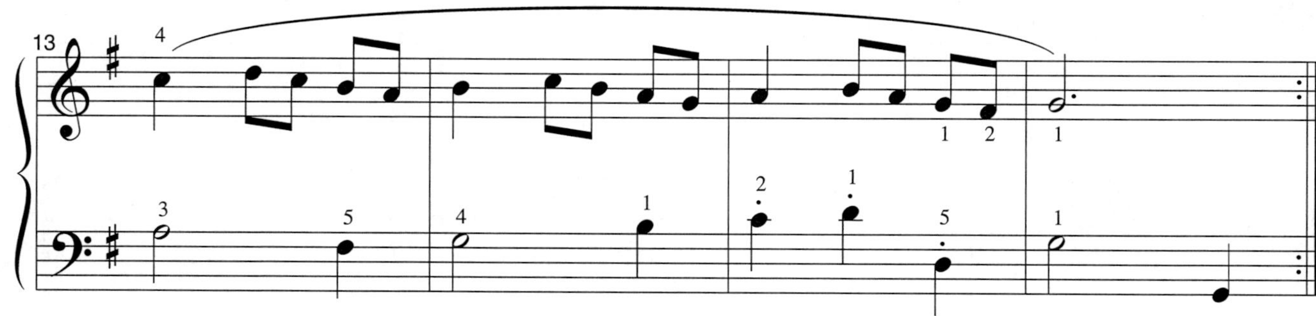

Minuet in G Minor

17
mf

21

25

29

Sonatina

Une Petit Chanson

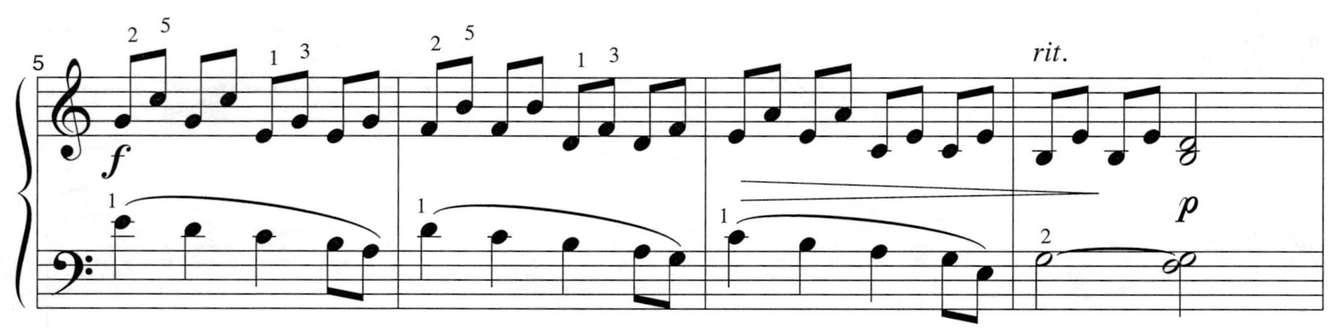

17
p
5 2 4 1
pp
3 5
2 4 5
1
21
4 2
mf
cresc.
1 2 1
2
5
25
f
1 1 1 1
rit.
pp
29
a tempo
p
4 4
33
decresc.
pp

Little Piano Piece, No. 2
(From *Six Little Piano Pieces*, Op. 19)

Arnold Schoenberg

Simple Gifts

Two Etudes

No. 1

C. Gurlitt, Op. 130, no. 1

Moderato

No. 2

C. Gurlitt, Op. 130, no. 2

Country Dance

From *For Children, Book I*, No. 6. Country Dance, 1909

Exotic Flowers

From *For Children, Book I*, No. 10. Exotic Flowers, 1909

Debbie Visits a Disco

13
mf
cresc. molto
16
ff
19
subito p
ff
mp
pp

Gymnopedie I
(Secondo)

Gymnopedie I
(Primo)

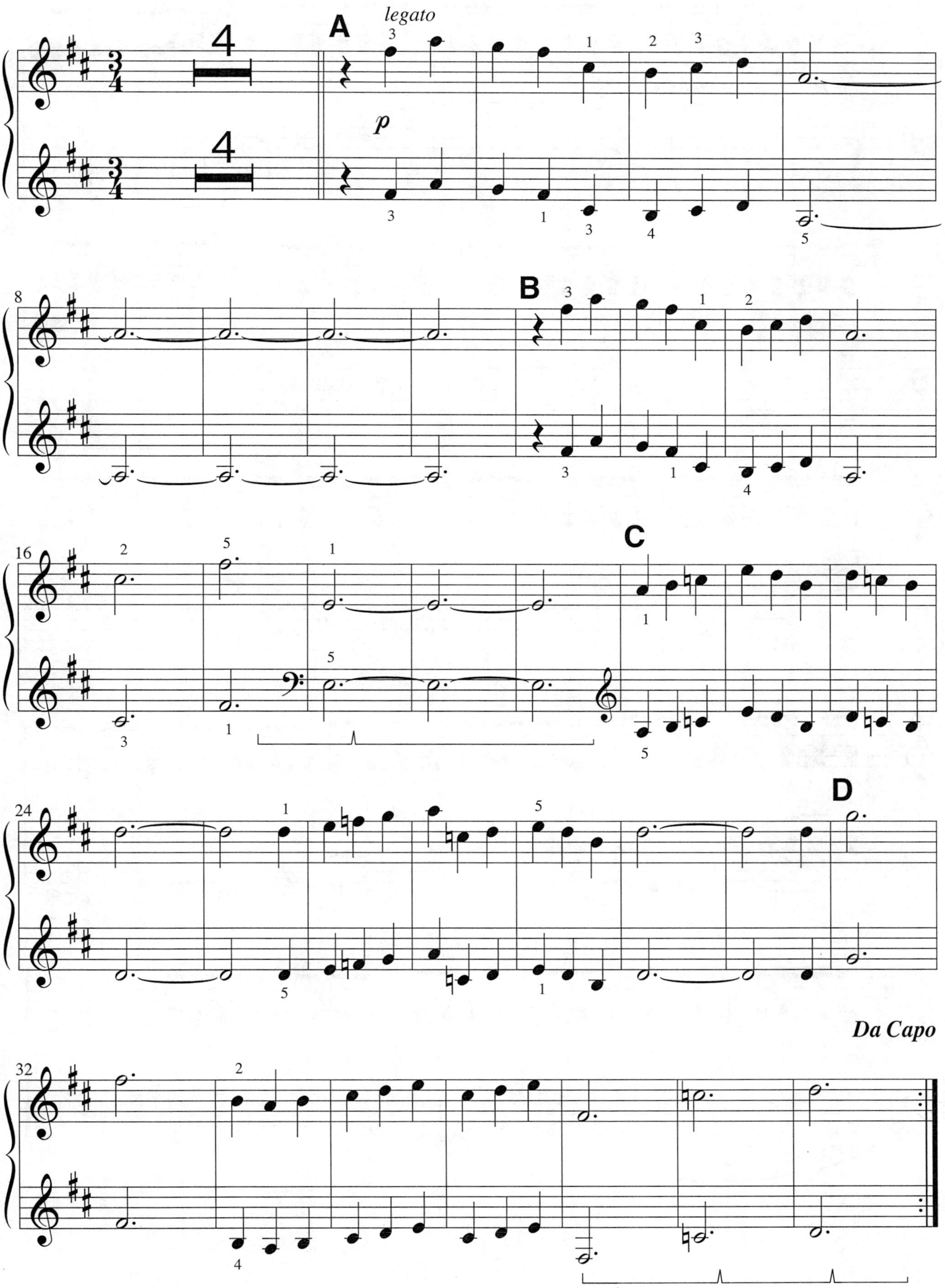

Allegro non troppo

Spanish Dance

Moderato

T. Oesten

My Country, 'Tis of Thee

Hymn to Joy

Root Position Triads

For Level Four piano, you will be required to play root position major, minor, augmented, and diminished triads on any note. Triads are constructed like this: Major triads -- Perfect 5th (P5) and a Major 3rd (M3); minor triads -- Perfect (P5) and a minor 3rd (m3); Augmented triads -- Augmented 5th (A5) and a Major 3rd (M3); Diminished triads -- diminished 5th (d5) and a minor 3rd (m3).

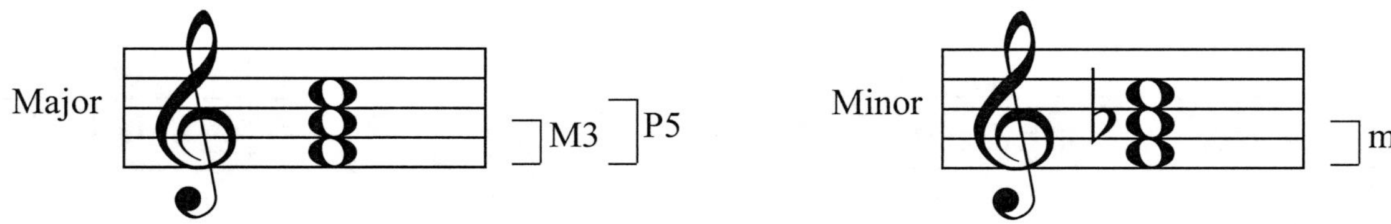

Use this fingering on all root position triads:

Right hand fingering: 1 3 5
Left hand fingering: 5 3 1

Here is the first set of triads (all the Major/minor triads on the white keys). If there is no accidental in front of a note then it should be considered a natural.

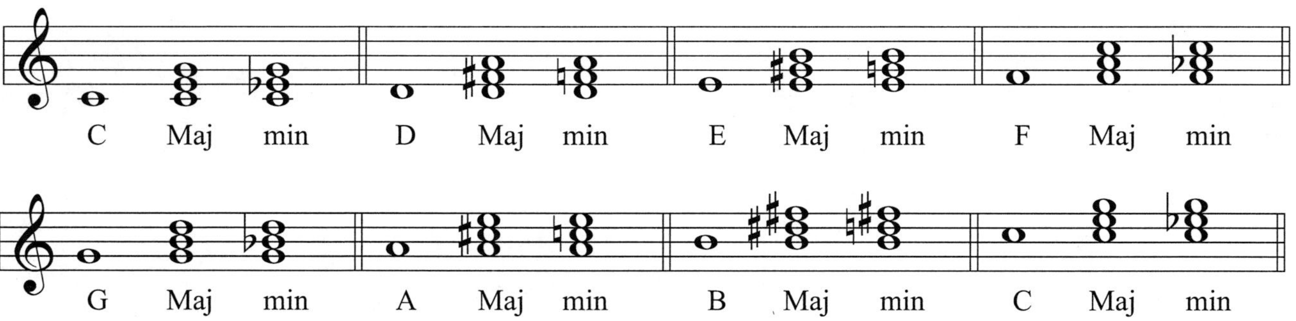

The next set of triads are all the Major/minor triads on the black notes. They are presented here in pairs, for example C#/D♭; D#/E♭, etc. For the purposes of actually playing the triad, it doesn't matter which version you use. For example, if A# Major triad seems complicated to you, then use its ENHARMONIC spelling, B♭ Major. If there is no accidental in front of a note then it should be considered a natural.

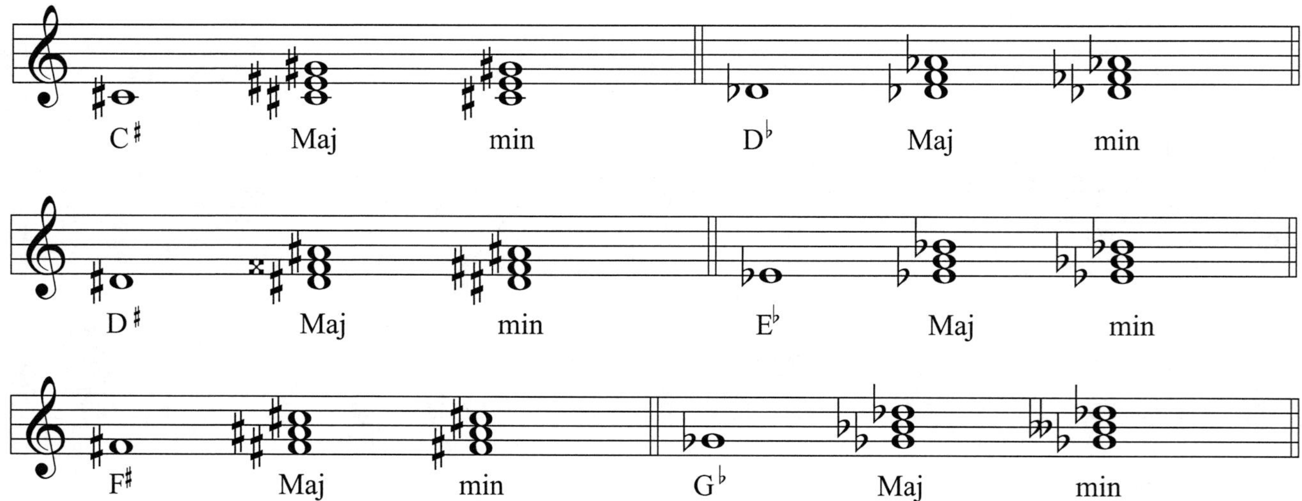

(Major/minor triads continued)

G♯
Maj
min
A♭
Maj
min
A♯
Maj
min
B♭
Maj
min

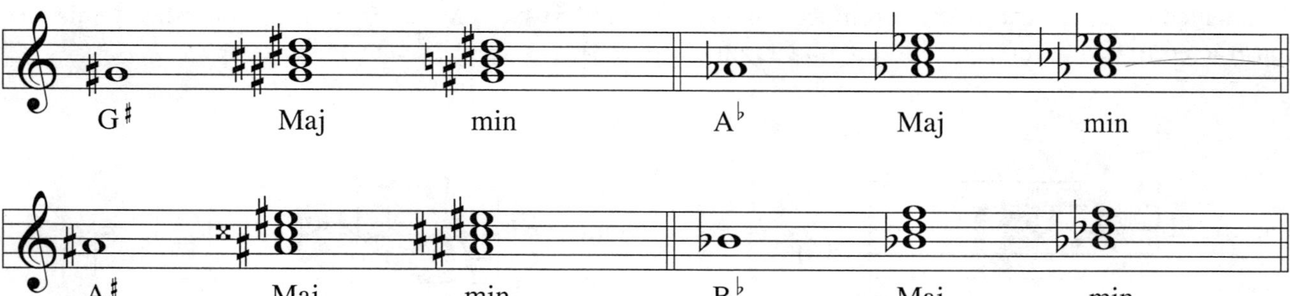

Here is a graphic representation of selected triads:

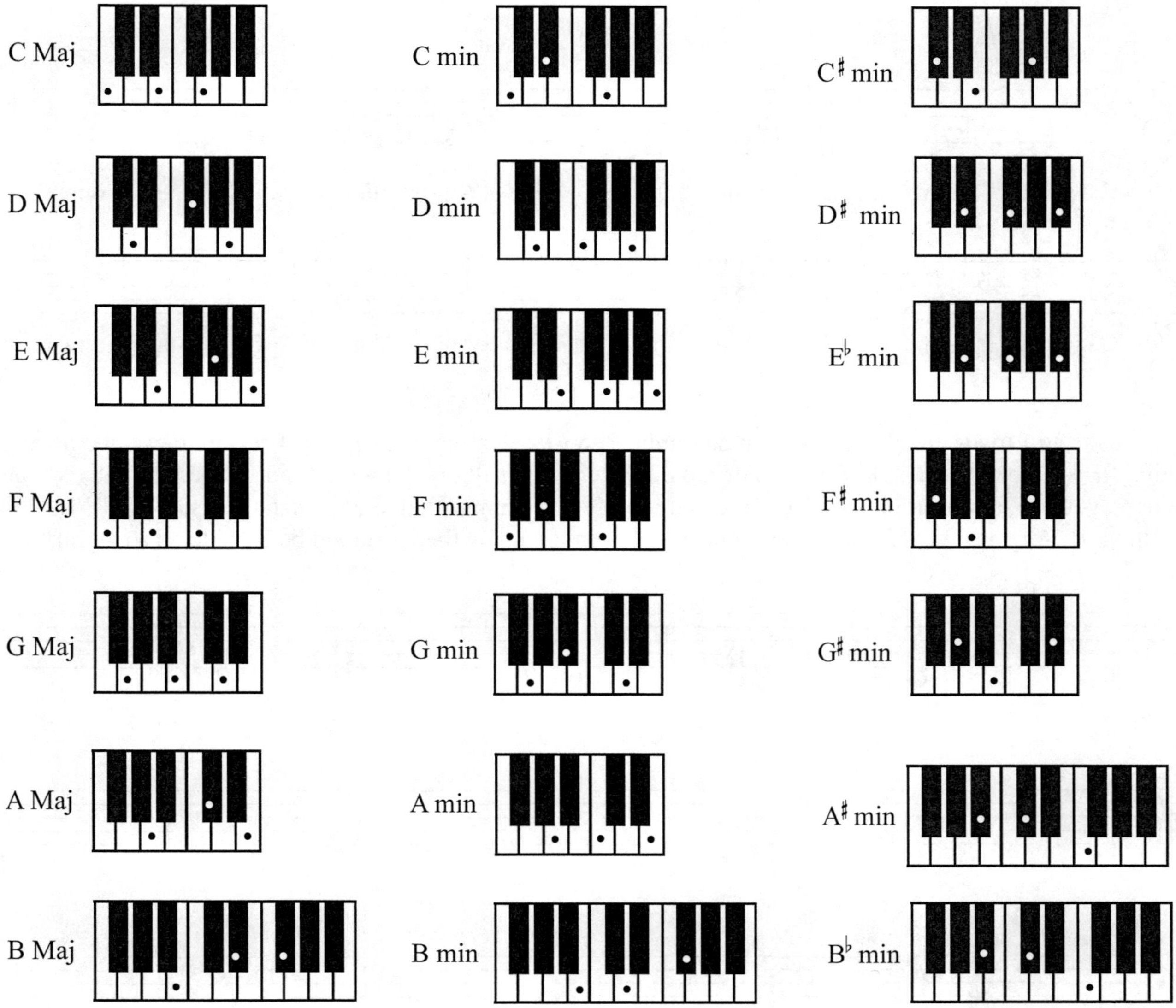

C Maj
C min
C♯ min
D Maj
D min
D♯ min
E Maj
E min
E♭ min
F Maj
F min
F♯ min
G Maj
G min
G♯ min
A Maj
A min
A♯ min
B Maj
B min
B♭ min

Root Position Triads, cont'd

Augmented triads are constructed from an Augmented 5th (A5) and a Major 3rd (M3); diminished triads are constructed from a diminished 5th (d5) and a minor 3rd (m3):

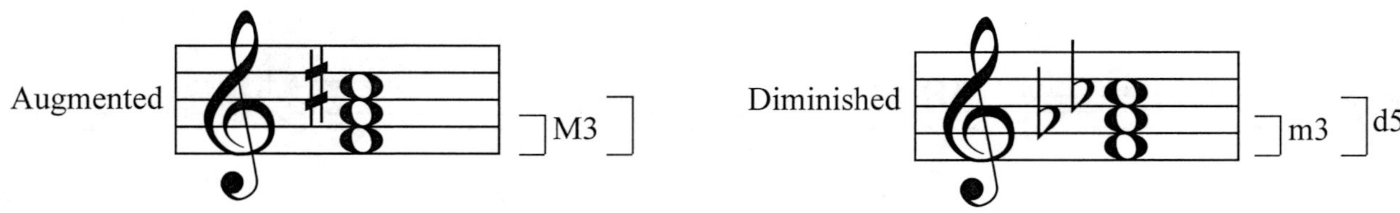

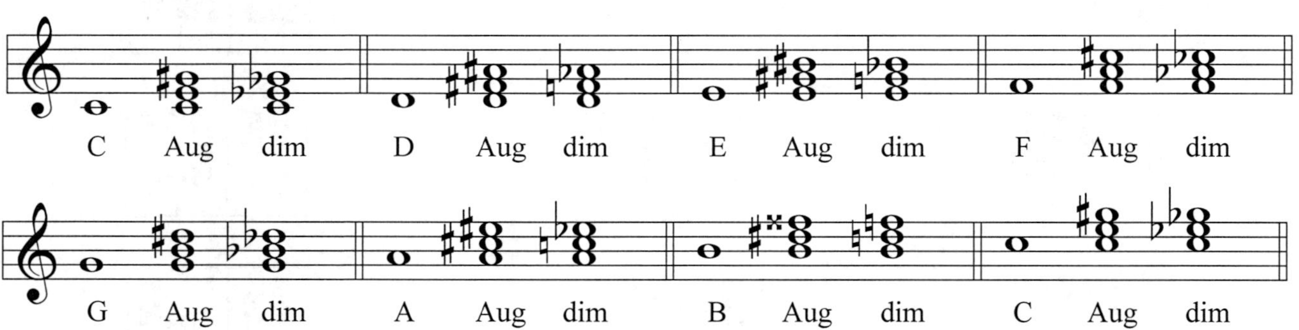

The final set of triads are all the Augmented/diminished triads on the black notes. They are presented here in pairs, for example: C#/D♭; D#/E♭, etc. For the purposes of actually playing the triad, it doesn't matter which version you use. For example, if A# Augmented triad seems complicated to you, then use its ENHARMONIC spelling, B♭ Augmented. If there is no accidental in front of a note then it should be considered a natural.

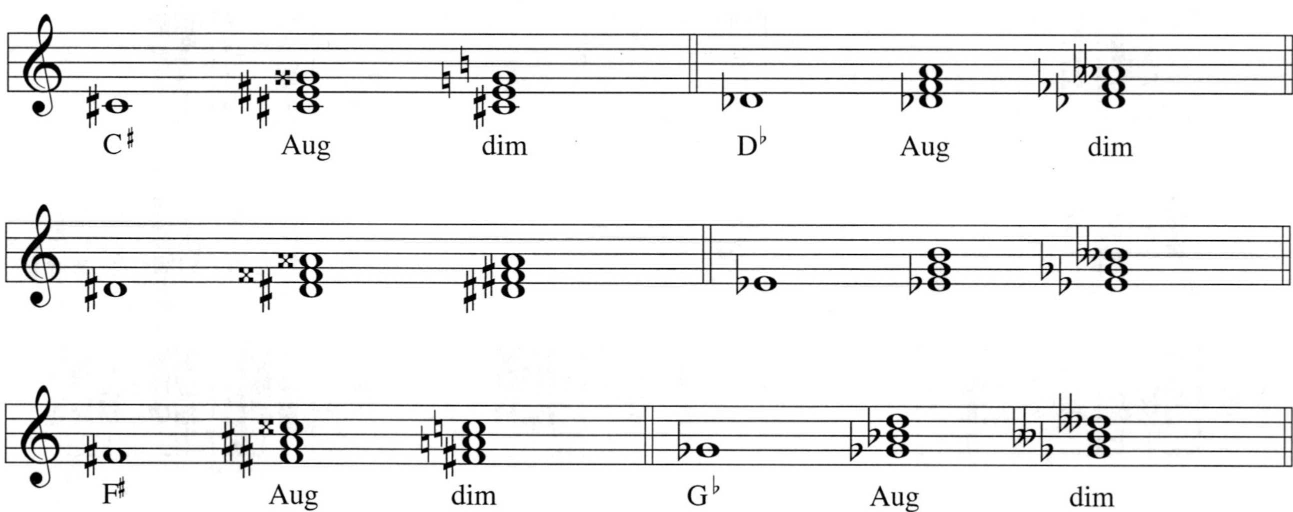

(Augmented/diminished triads continued)

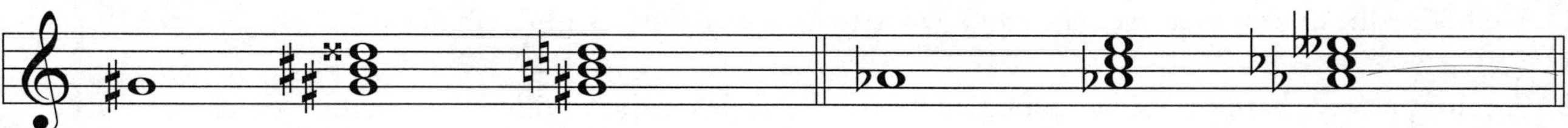

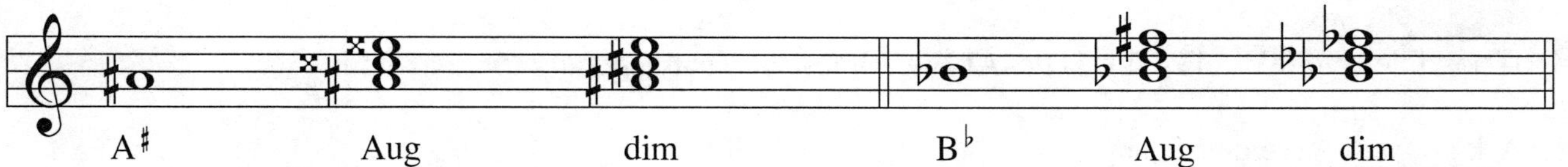

Here is a graphic representation of selected Augmented and diminished triads:

C Aug	C dim	C♯ Aug
D Aug	D dim	D♯ dim
E Aug	E Aug	E♭ Aug
F Aug	F dim	F♯ dim
G Aug	G dim	G♯ dim
A Aug	A dim	A♯ Aug
B Aug	B dim	B♭ dim

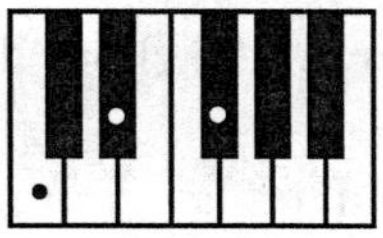

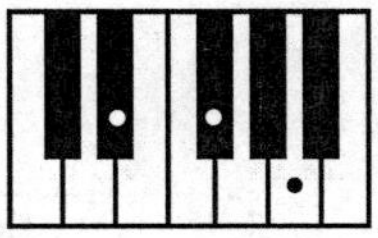

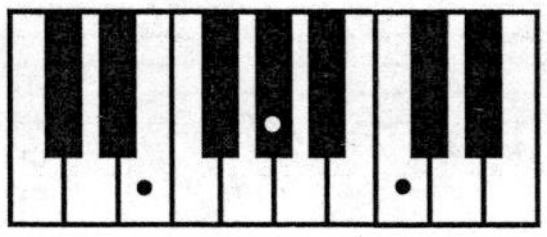

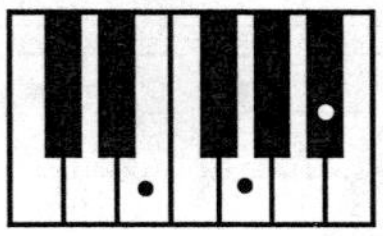

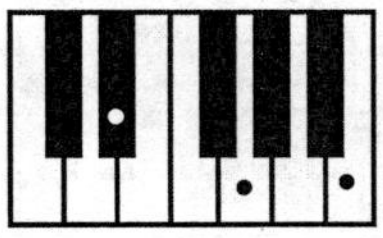

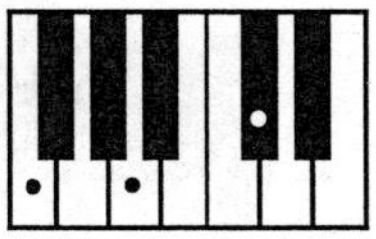

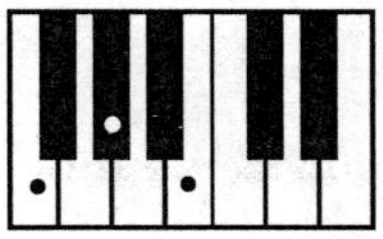

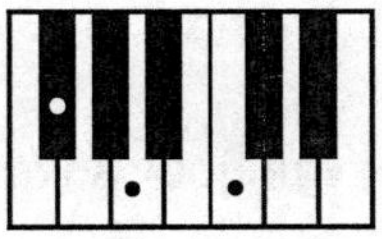

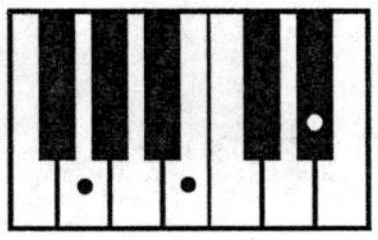

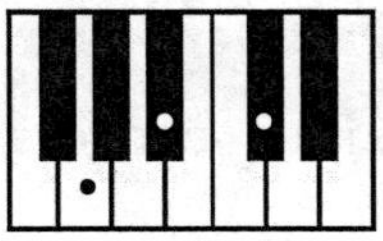

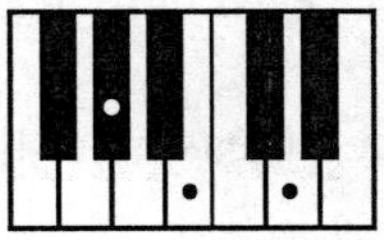

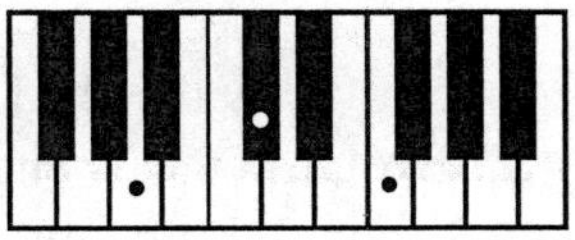

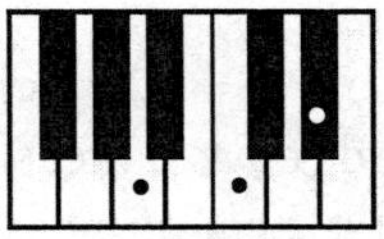

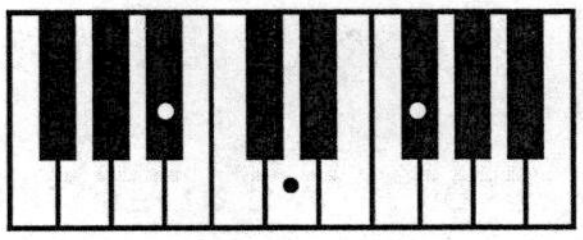

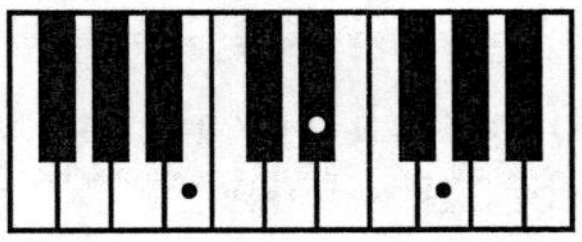

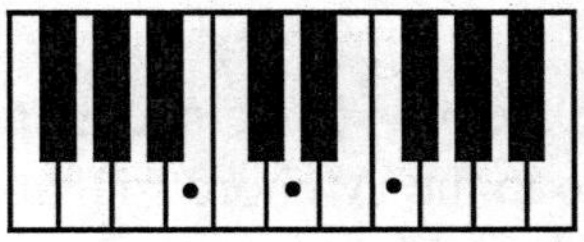

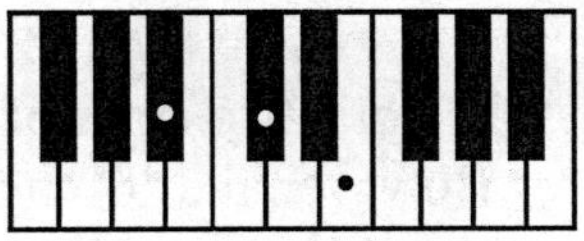

Procedures for Harmonizing Melodies

1. Memorize the appropriate cadence and be able to play it in the key of the melody.

2. For now, always harmonize the second degree of the scale (major or minor key) with a V7 chord.

3. In most cases, the 1st and last chord of the melody will alwasy be a I (i) chord.

4. If possible, avoid V^7 - IV. This is not ALWAYS possible, but generally try to avoid it.

5. Ask yourself these questions:

   a. Is the melody note I'm trying to harmonize in the chord I'm trying to use? If it isn't then it probably won't work. (See: Appendix IV: Non-Chord Tones.)

   b. Does the shape of the melody suggest a specific chord? If the melody outlines a specific triad or seventh chord then that is a good indication for the chord that should be used.

6. Write in the symbols for the chords you intend to play. For now, only use the chord voicings of the cadences you practiced.

In the above melody segment, make the following observations:

   - The HARMONIC RHYTHM is a half note (see below).

   - The first measure outlines the I chord. Also, it's a good idea to always start with the I chord.

   - The first two beats of the second measure outlines part of the IV chord.

   - The "G" on beat three is not in the IV chord but IS in the I chord or the V^7 chord . If you use the I chord you can go to either I or V^7 for the next chord (beat 1, measure 3). However, if you use the V^7 chord, you HAVE to also use the V^7 chord for the 1st beat of measure 3 (see rule # 3 above). Probably it's best to use the I chord.

   - The first two notes of measure three are both contained in the V^7 chord, so that is a logical choice. However, the "f" on beat one is also in the IV chord so that would work too. If you use the IV chord on beat 1 then the "G" on the "and" of beat 2 becomes an "escape" tone and THAT'S OK even though it's not in the IV chord. See: **Appendix IV: Non-Chord Tones**.

- The first beat of measure four is the second degree of the scale. Therefore, it is automatically harmonized by the V^7 chord (rule #2 above). The last note of measure four is in the I chord and it's generally a good idea to harmonize the final note of a melody with the I chord.

IN GENERAL:

- You may harmonize each melody note one at a time, or . . .
- You may harmonize the melody using a strict "harmonic rhythm." See the above example.

HARMONIC RHYTHM means:

"A rhythmically strict progression of chords." In the above example the harmonic rhythm is a half note (one chord every two beats). The harmonic rhythm may be anything that sounds good. However, the best harmonic rhythm depends upon such factors as tempo, style, etc. A typical harmonic rhythm would be either one or two chords per measure. Also, tempo affects decisions regarding the harmonic rhythm. Generally, if the tempo is fast then use a slower harmonic rhythm. If the tempo is slow then use a faster harmonic rhythm.

Here's a harmonized version of the melody on the previous page written out as you might play it using the simple cadence chord voicings:

Here's another version using the same chords but implementing one of the accompaniment patterns:

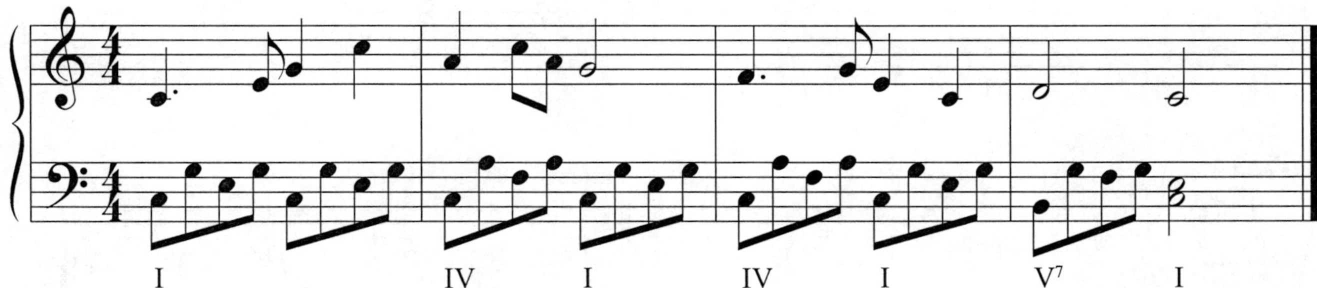

Try playing the above melody using one of the other accompaniment patterns.

For more DETAILED information regarding harmonizing melodies, please see Appendix 2: Melodic Phrases and Appendix 3: Melodic Cadences.

Block-Chord Cadences

"Block-chord" means all chords are **voiced** with 3 notes in each hand and each chord is identified by its Roman Numeral, not by its inversion. The following are "block-chord" style cadences. Here, "cadence" means a succession of chords (such as I-IV-I-V7-I) and does not refer to what happes at the end of a phrase as described in Appendix 3 (page 110).

* The actual figured bass would be expressed: I   IV$^6_4$ I   V$^6_5$ I

Cadences, cont'd: V^7/V

* The actual figured bass would be expressed: I   IV$^6_4$ I   V$^4_2$/V   V   V$^6_5$ I

Accompaniment Patterns

One way to harmonize a melody is to use the BLOCK-CHORDS from the cadences on the previous pages. However, a more interesting accompaniment can be accomplished by superimposing patterns on the block-chords as demonstrated below. In each example 1-4, the top staff shows the block chord and the bottom staff shows how to superimpose the accompaniment pattern.

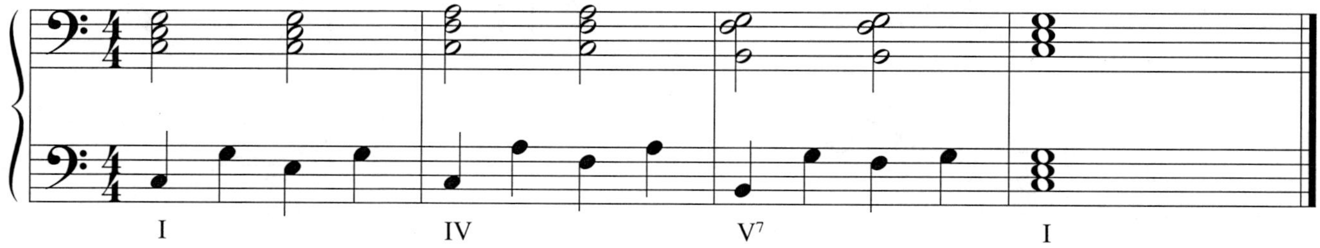

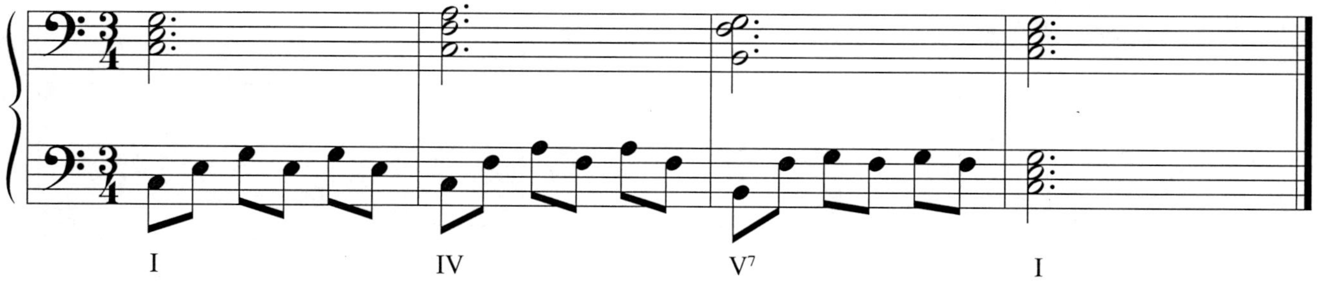

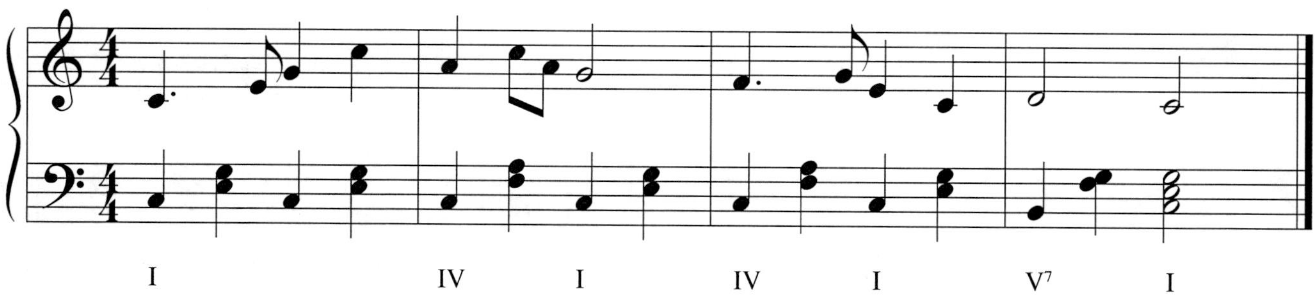

Here's an actual melody written out using Accompaniment Pattern #1

Melodies for Harmonization

WDL
6
Harmonize each melody note.
HAMBURG
Lowell Mason, 1824
7
WDL
8
LIGHTLY ROW
Folk Song
9
LOW DUTCH
Bay Psalm Book, 1698 edition
Harmonize each melody note - skiw tempo
10

Folk Song
11
WDL
12
NINETY-FIFTH
Wyeth's, Repository of Sacred Music, Part 2nd, 1820
13
Folk Song
14
Be Creative.
WDL
15

MELODY
Robert Schumann
16
BLUE SKY
American Folk Song
= 1st time. 2nd time harmonize each melody note.
17
WALTZ
Franz Schubert
18
Folk Song
19

MINUET
J. S. Bach
20
HOLY MANA
Kentucky Harmony, 1825
21
FOLK SONG
22
Harmonize beats one and three
AMAZING GRACE
Virginia Harmony, 1831
23

56
DARK EYES
Hungarian Folk Song
24
SHE'LL BE COMIN' ROUND THE MOUNTAIN
American Folk Song
25
WALTZ
Folk Song
26
REAPER'S SONG
Robert Schumann
27
FOUNDATION
Union Harmony, 1837
28

ST. MAGNUS
Jeremiah Clark
29
from Don Giovanni
W.A. Mozart
30
American Folk Song
31
WDL
32
French Folk Song
33

GO TELL IT ON THE MOUNTAIN
Negro Spiritual
34
AURA LEE
American Folk Song
35
STREETS OF LOREDO
American Folk Song
36
HAPPY FARMER
Robert Schumann
37

FORREST GREEN
English Folk Song
38
HOME ON THE RANGE
American Folk Song
39
WE SHALL OVERCOME
Negro Spiritual
40
German Folk Song
41

Improvisation

The goal for improvisation skills in Secondary Piano is to improvise simple melodies over a given chord progression. In Level Two the improvisation examples will consist of:

1. Primary chords and one secondary dominant (V7/V) in major and minor keys through two accidentals.
2. Improvised melodies should consist of chord tones, passing tones and neighbor tones.
3. The range of the improvisation should be about a 5th (for example, use scale degrees 1 - 5).
4. Improvised melodies should generally make use of a RHYTHMIC MOTIVE.
5. Non-motivic construction concepts will be introduced.
6. Use a consistent HARMONIC RHYTHM (for example, 1 or 2 chords per measure).

Improvisation involves spontaneously making up a melody over a given chord progression. The chord voicings required in Level 2 piano will be the same as those found in the bock-chord cadences earlier in this book. If you need to review the differences between chord tones and non-chord tones, see **Appendix IV** for a detailed explanation. All the improvisation examples in Level 2 piano will involve improvising melodies consisting of a combination of chord tones and non-chord tones. Here is a written-out example demonstrating basic requirements for this level:

Consider the following example:

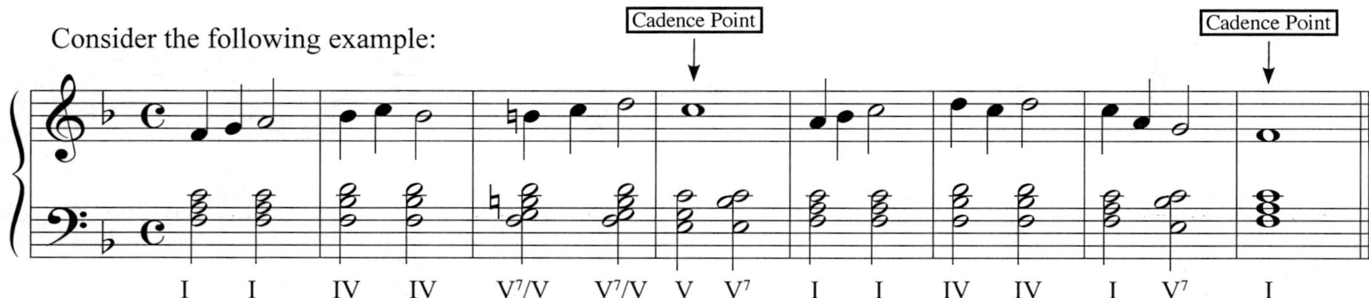

In the above example the melody notes consist of chord tones, passing tones, and neighbor tones. Note the use of the secondary dominant V7/V in measure 3 and how it resolves. At a cadence, V7/V should resolve to a V chord and then the V should progress to the V7 chord. Also notice how the rhythm for the melody is the same in each measure except for the whole notes in measures 4 and 8. This repetitive rhythm is called a "rhythm motive" and the whole notes in measures 4 and 8 are at CADENCE POINTS (see Appendix 2 and 3 at the end of this book for a detailed explanation of melodic phrases and cadences). A MOTIVE is a short melodic and/ or rhythmic idea used as a constructional element. In other words, a MOTIVIC IDEA is used over and over again to build up a larger section or an entire composition. Also, notice how the rhythmic motive is spread out (superimposed) over 2 adjacent chords.

The short example above is a complete melody and consists of TWO PHRASES. The PHRASES are set apart by the whole notes in measures 4 and 8 and these POINTS OF REST within the melody are called CADENCES. It is often easy to find the CADENCE POINTS in any melody -- just look for the longest note values, particularly if they occur in groups of 4 or 8 measures. FOUR-MEASURE PHRASES are very common in all styles of Western music. You can make your improvised melodies sound like "real" melodies if you structure them like REAL MELODIES:

1. Use a simple rhythmic motive.
2. Use LONG NOTES (whole notes, dotted whole notes, etc.) at the cadence points.
3. Superimpose your rhythmic motive of TWO consecutive chords.

4. Always end with the tonic note (1st degree of the scale). The majority of successful melodies in western music end on the tonic note. "Successful melodies" are those melodies which have been IN USE for a long period of time, for example, 50 years, 100 years, etc. Look through the melodies in the Harmonized Melodies section of this book and you will discover that they ALL end on the tonic note.

The goal for Level II Piano is to be able to improvise using chord tones, passing tones, and neighbor tones over a given chord progression. Try improvising a melody over the following chords. The first measure has been done for you and you should use this rhythmic MOTIVE in each measure throughout the example except at the cadence points where you see the whole notes.

Improvise a melody for the following example using the rhythmic motive in first measure. Repeat in the keys of C and F. Use long notes (whole notes) at the cadence points.

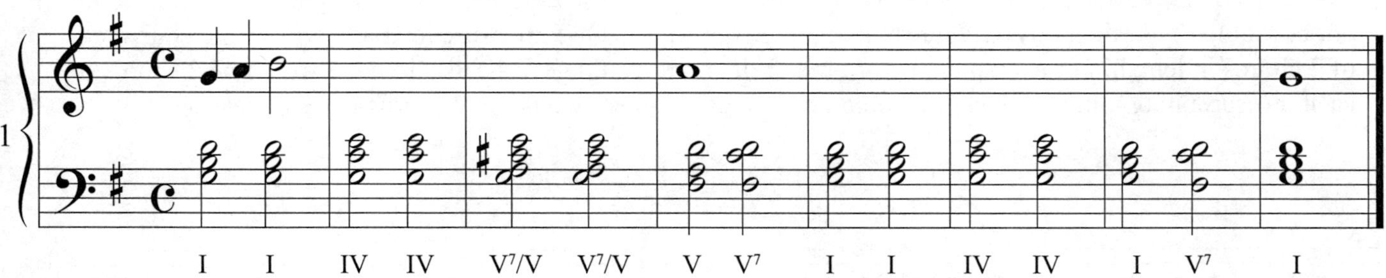

Do:

1. Use chord tones, passing tones, and neighbor tones. If you need to, consult the example on the previous page.
2. Generally, keep the overall range of your improvisation within about a 5th or 6th. You may want to start out with a limited range of a 3rd and then gradually increase the range to 5th or 6th.
3. If you have trouble with the coordination aspect, try "patting" the rhythm of the right hand while you play the chords in the left hand. It's always a good idea to practice counting outloud while you play.
4. Try starting your improvisation on a scale degree other than the 1st scale degree (for example the 3rd of the 5th).

Don't:

1. Don't write out your improvisation. Make it up (improvise it) every time.

When you feel comfortable playing the example above in the written key of F major, try playing it in the keys of C major and G major.

Improvise a melody for the following example using the rhythmic motive in first measure. Repeat in the keys of C and G. Use long notes (whole notes) at the cadence points.

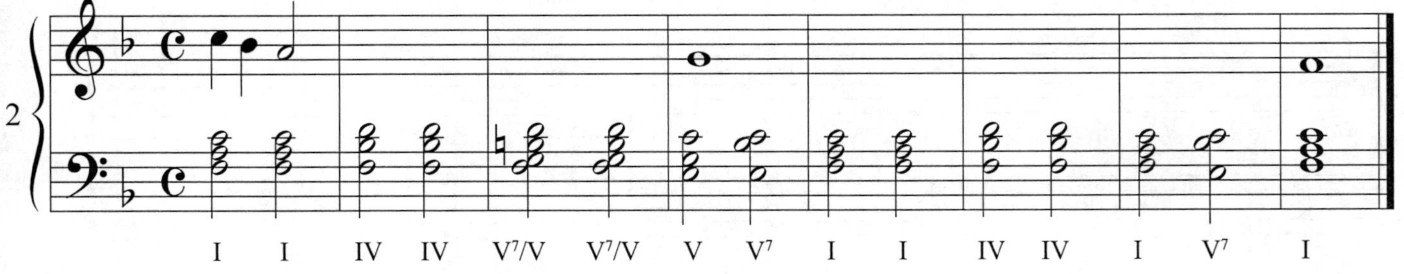

Improvisation, Part II: More on Rhythmic Motives

As described earlier, a MOTIVE is a short melodic and/or rhythmic idea used as a constructional element. Many successful melodies use non-motivic melodic construction. However, the efforts of novice improvisers to play non-motivic improvisations often sound "rambling" -- that is, the improvised melody rambles in an almost random way, not having any real sense of direction, strong cadence points, or any sense of tension/relaxation or climax. A melody or improvisation will have a greater sense of unity and direction (including climax and cadence) if it is constructed motivically, especially for someone just learning to improvise.

To begin to develop a good concept of rhythmic motive, write out four (4) one-measure rhythmic motives for each of the meters below. Individual melody notes are inconsequential at this point. The actual melody notes will later be determined by the given chords. For now, use any pitches you want or just use one pitch. To be a VIABLE rhythmic motive, your rhythmic motive must have at least TWO different rhythmic values, for example a half note and 2 quarter notes. Consequently, 4 quarter notes, 2 half notes, 8 eighth notes, etc. would not be viable rhythmic motives. Your rhythmic motives will be ONE measure long and will be the equivalent of 2 chords in length. For example, in 4/4/ time each chord would get 2 beats and there would be 2 chords in each measure; in 6/4 time each chord would get 3 beats and there would be 2 chords in each measure.

After you have completed the composition of your rhythmic motives, improvise complete melodies over the example chord progressions below by making use of one of your motives. Use ONE motive for the entire improvisation. Use a LONG note (dotted whole note) at the cadence points. Before you begin, analyze the chords and write them in the music below the chords. DO NOT WRITE OUT YOUR IMPROVISATION IN THE MUSIC, but you may sketch out your chosen rhythmic motive in the provided treble clef.

Improvisation: Improvised Melodies Over Chord Symbols -- Review

When you improvise melodies over chord progressions the voicings of the chords you play in the left hand should be the same as the cadence chords you have already learned. However, if your instructor agrees you may use any voicings you wish as long as you keep the rhythm correct and the tempo steady.

Practice the examples in the required keys for your cadences (through 2 accidentals. Each example is two phrases (2 lines) long. The next-to-last chord in each phrase is the "CADENCE POINT." Please follow these rules:

1. Play the cadence for the key in which you plan to improvise.
2. Play through the chord progression with just the left hand using the cadence voicings.
3. Use one of the rhythmic motives you wrote out on the previous page.
4. Play the chord progression with your left hand while you PAT the rhythmic motive with your right.
5. Play LONG notes (one note that lasts for 2 chords) at all the CADENCE POINTS.
6. Keep the range of your improvisation within a 5th or 6th (although you might start off with a range of a 3rd or 4th).
7. Create your improvisation using chord tones, passing tones and neighbor tones.
8. Generally, it is better to use more steps than skips.
9, Always end the improvisation on the tonic note.

For all these chord progressions:

#1
| I | I | IV | IV | I | I | V^7 | V^7 |
| I | I | IV | IV | I | V^7 | I | I |

1. Prepare each one TWICE: once with 2 beats for each chord and once with 3 beats for each chord.

#2
| i | i | iv | iv | i | i | V^7 | V^7 |
| i | i | iv | iv | i | V^7 | i | i |

2. Use one of the rhythmic motives you composed on the previous page.

3. The CADENCE POINT for each phrase is the next-to-last chord in each line. So, play a LONG note on that chord and don't continue your rhythmic motive. See the example at the beginning of this section as a model.

#3
| I | V^7 | I | I | IV | IV | V^7 | V^7 |
| I | IV | I | I | IV | V^7 | I | I |

4. It's always a good idea to practice playing the chords with the left hand while you PAT your rhythmic motive with the right hand.

#4
| i | V^7 | i | i | iv | iv | V^7 | V^7 |
| i | iv | i | i | iv | V^7 | i | i |

Improvisation, Part III: Non-Motivic Melodic Construction.

Creating a successful non-motivic improvisation is more challenging than using motivic construction. Here
are a few basic principles which will help in improvising non-motivic melodies.

Consider the following examples:

The first melody, COME SUNDAY (composed in 1946 by Duke Ellington), is constructed non-motivically.
The second melody, SONG 13 (composed in 1623 by Orlando Gibbons), makes use of motivic construction.
Both melodies consist of four phrases and both melodies use longer note values at the cadence points. COME
SUNDAY has more rhythmic diversity and this is the key to constructing interesting and effective melodies which
do not make use of motivic construction. THE MOST INTERESTING NON-MOTIVIC MELODIES ARE
THOSE WHICH HAVE RHYTHMIC DIVERSITY, that is, different rhythmic combinations in each measure.

The absolute opposite of this are melodies which use only a single rhythmic value throughout, as in the following
melody.

ST. ANNE has proved to be one of the most successful melodies ever written despite its static rhythm. However, what it lacks in rhythmic diversity it makes up in strong cadence points, interesting intervals and climax. The melodic interval of a 4th is used 8 times throughout the tune and this tends to reinforce a strong sense of cadence. In addition, the overall angular intervallic motion (a descending interval followed by an ascending interval) gives a unique feel to the tune which makes it memorable.

Here are some general guidelines for creating tunes which are not constructed motivically:

1. Strive for rhythmic diversity (different rhythms in each measure)
2. Have clearly defined cadence points. The melody note at the actual cadence point should be the longest note value of the phrase.
3. The melody should have a sense of climax. Often this is accomplished with the highest note of the melody occurring only once at the point of climax.

Points 2 and 3 above also apply to motivic melodies but are particularly true for non-motivic melodies. Otherwise, there is a strong tendency for non-motivic melodies to degenerate into rambling bits of nonsense.

Improvise non-motivic melodies over the given chord progressions below. Before you begin, analyze the chords and write them in the music below the chords. <u>DO NOT</u> WRITE OUT YOUR IMPROVISATION IN THE MUSIC, but you may sketch out rhythmic ideas in the provided treble clef.

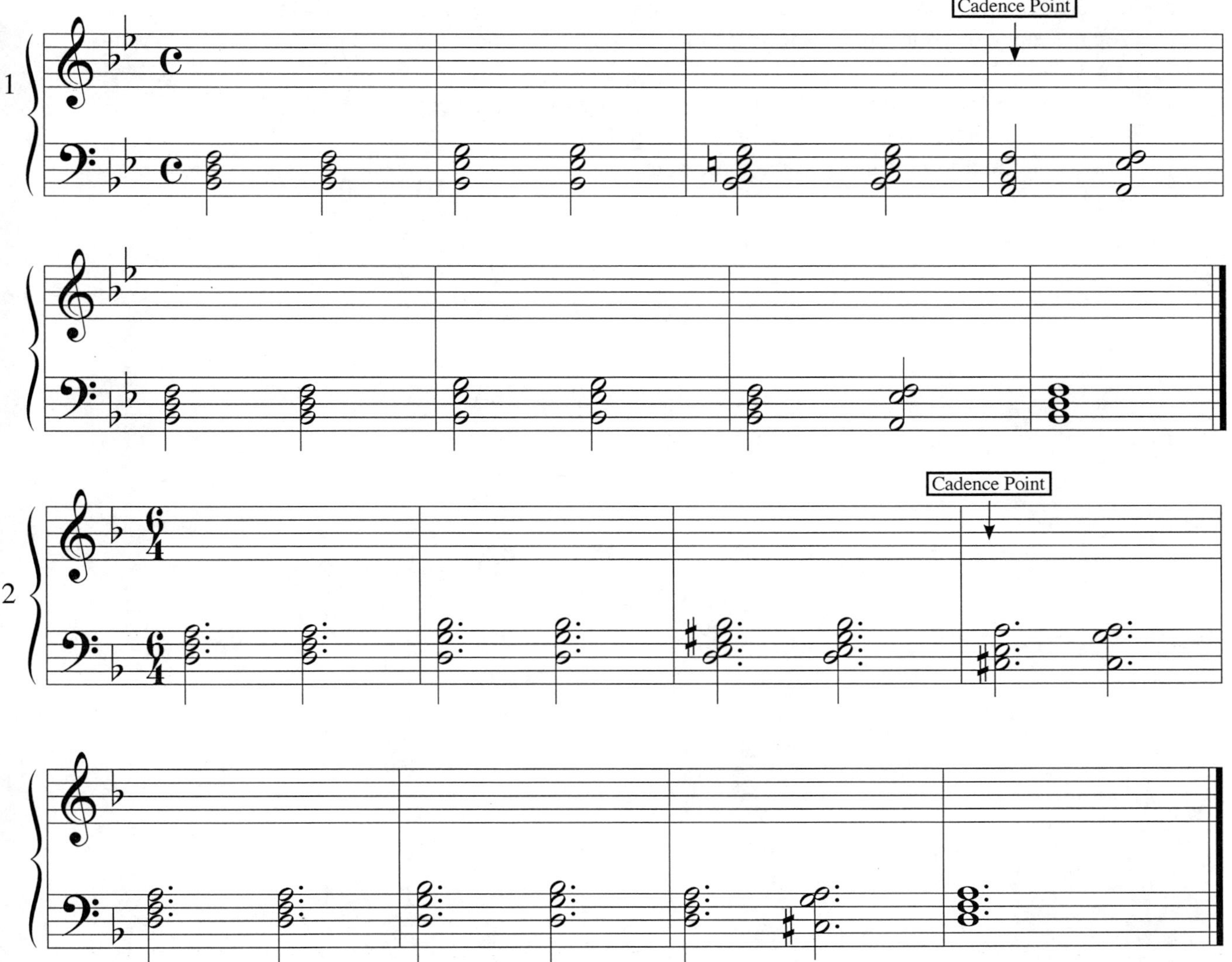

Improvisation, Part IV: More Improvised Melodies Over Chord Symbols
Secondary Dominants: V^7/V

Improvise melodies over the following chord progressions using any combination of techniques you have learned so far. The voicings you should use for the chords are the same voicings you have learned for the cadences earlier in this book. However, if your instructor agrees you may use any voicing you wish as long as you keep the rhythm correct and the tempo steady. For example, give each chord the correct number of beats.

Play each example in the following keys:

> Major: C D F G B^b
> Minor: am bm dm em gm

Each example is two phrases (2 lines) long. You should prepare each improvisation twice: once giving each chord 2 beats, and once giving each chord 3 beats.

Please follow these procedures:

1. Play the cadence for the key in which you plan to improvise.
2. Play through the chord progression with just the left hand using the cadence voicings.
3. Use one of the rhythmic motives you wrote out earlier in this section.
4. Play the chord progression with your left hand while you PAT the rhythmic motive with your right.
5. Play LONG notes (one note that lasts for 2 chords) at all the CADENCE POINTS.
6. Keep the range of your improvisation within a 5th or 6th (although you might start off with a range of a 3rd or 4th).
7. Create your improvisation using chord tones, passing tones and neighbor tones.
8. Generally, it is better to use more steps than skips.
9, Always end the improvisation on the tonic note

Cadence Point

1

I	I	IV	IV	I	V^7/V	V	V^7
I	I	IV	IV	I	V^7	I	I

2

i	i	iv	iv	i	V^7/V	V	V^7
i	i	iv	iv	i	V^7	i	i

3

I	IV	I	I	IV	V^7/V	V	V^7
I	V^7/V	V	V^7	I	V^7	I	I

4

i	iv	i	i	iv	V^7/V	V	V^7
i	V^7/V	V	V^7	i	V^7	i	i

5

I	IV	V^7	I	V	V^7/V	V	V^7
I	V^7/V	V	V^7/V	V	V^7	I	I

Class Notes

Sight Reading and Transposition I: Piano Scores

WDL
9
WDL
10
WDL
11

WDL
12
JINGLE BELLS
Carol
13
MERRILY WE ROLL ALONG
American Folk Song
14

WDL
15
MY LORD, WHAT A MORNING
arr. by WDL
16
ST. FLAVIAN
17

SONATINA
WDL

LIGHTLY ROW
arr. by WDL

DUET IN G MINOR
WDL
20
ODE TO JOY
Beethoven, arr. WDL
21

HAMBURG
Lowell Mason
22
CANON 1
WDL
23
CANON 2
WDL
24
GERMAN DANCE
Beethoven
25

ETUDETTÉ
WDL
26
MINUET
G. Telemann
27
MY LORD, WHAT A MORNING
arr. WDL
28

MELODY
R. SCHUMANN

DANCE
Béla Bartók, ca. 1910

from *Don Giovanni*, by W.A. Mozart
arr. WDL

Sight Reading and Transposition II: Open Scores

from *Gloria*
Antonio Vivaldi

1

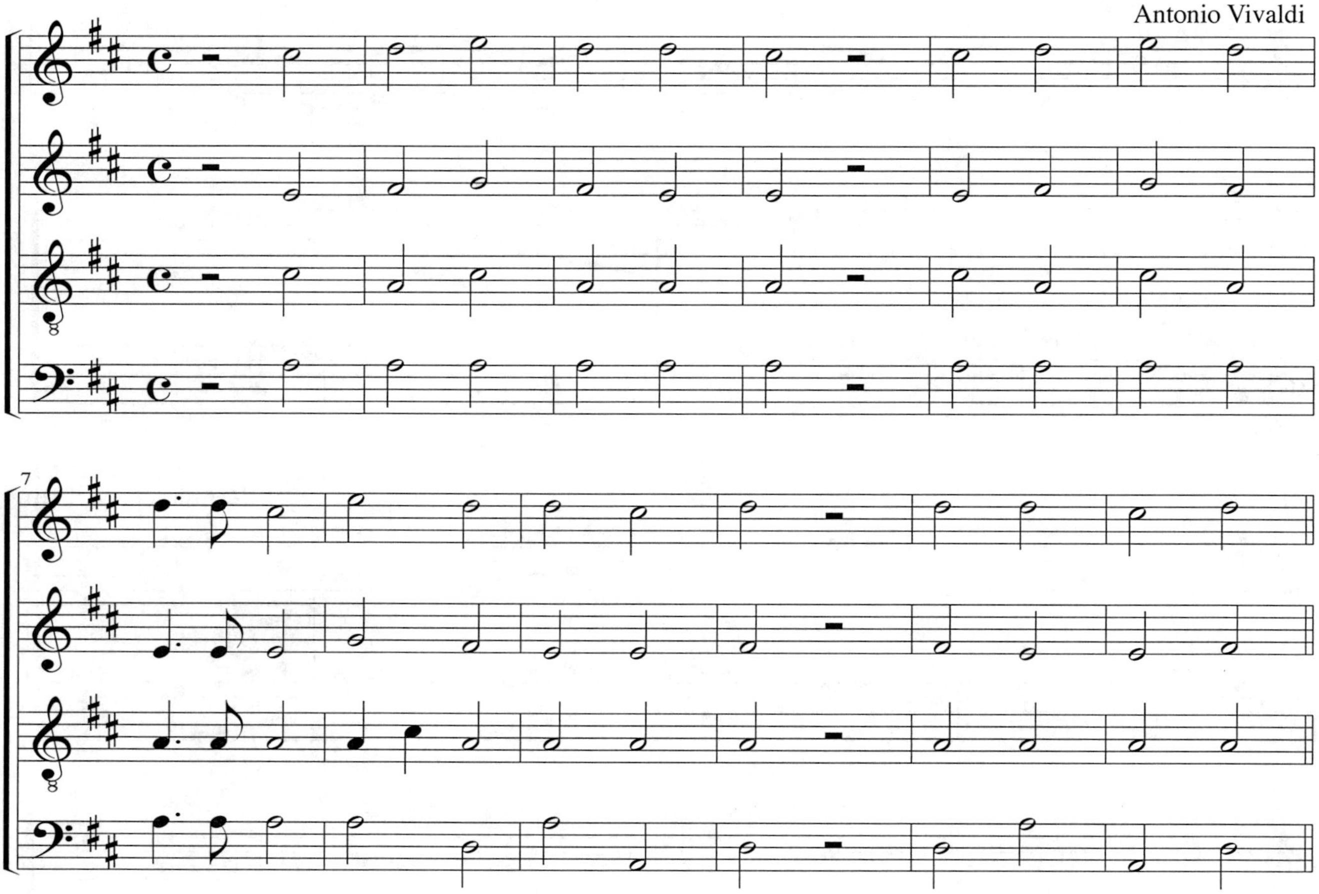

Anonymous
c. 1600

2

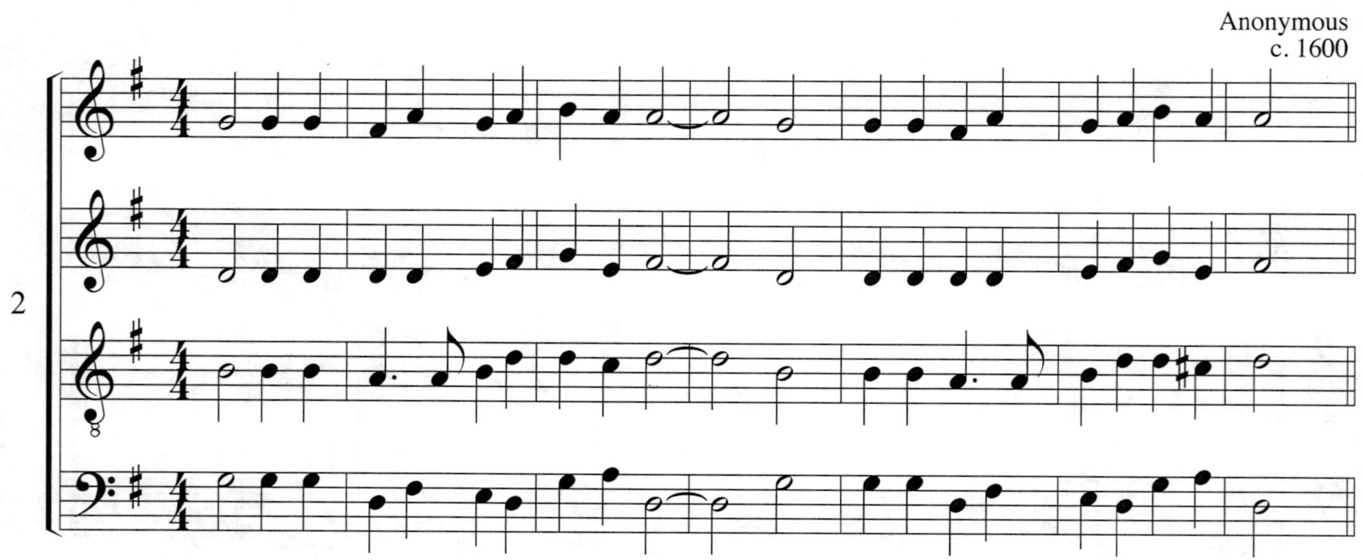

Ave Maria
Jacob Arcadelt

3

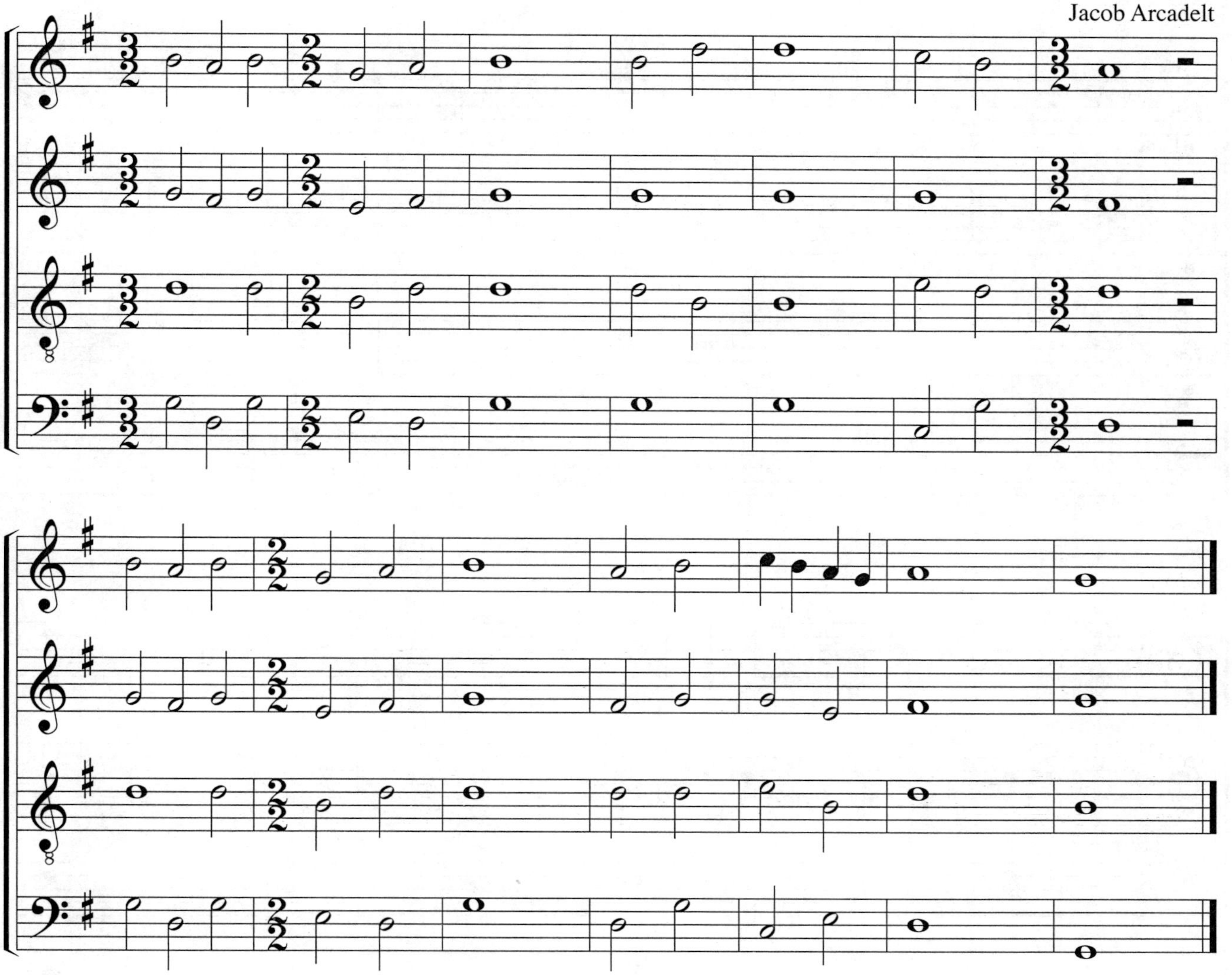

IN BABILONE
Traditional Dutch Melody

4

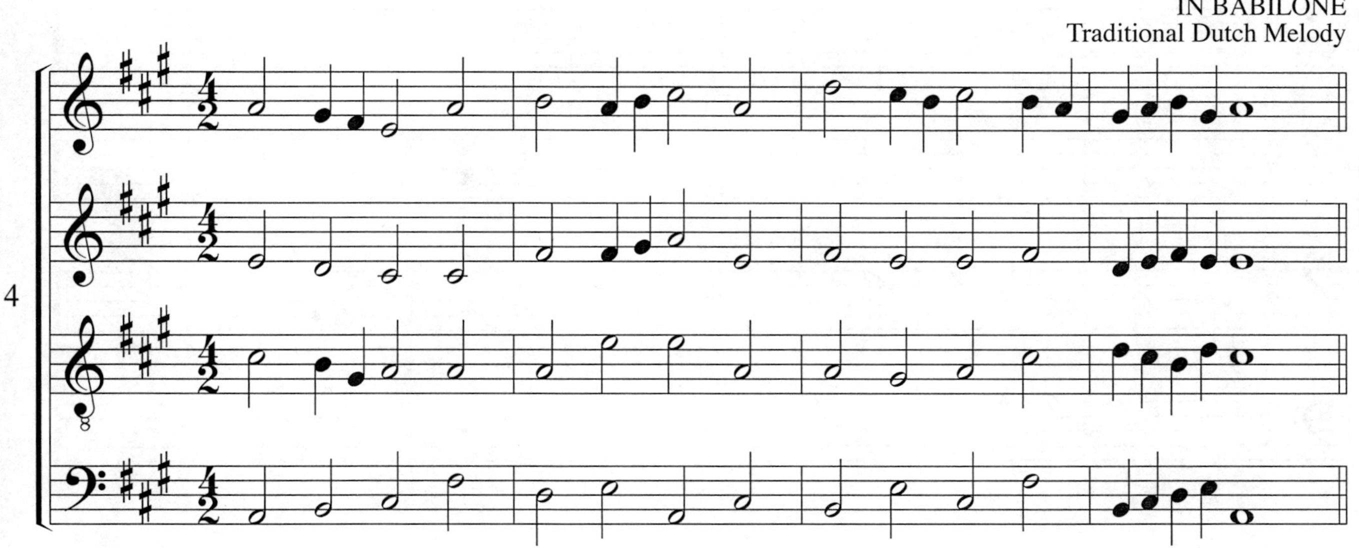

G.F. Handel
5

from Cosi fan Tutti
W.A. Mozart
6

Canzon
Wm. Brade

7

from Christmas Oratorio
Saint-Saëns

8

Trio
Bernardo Pisano
9
7

Lo, How a Rose e'er Blooming
Michael Praetorius
10

Open Score #11

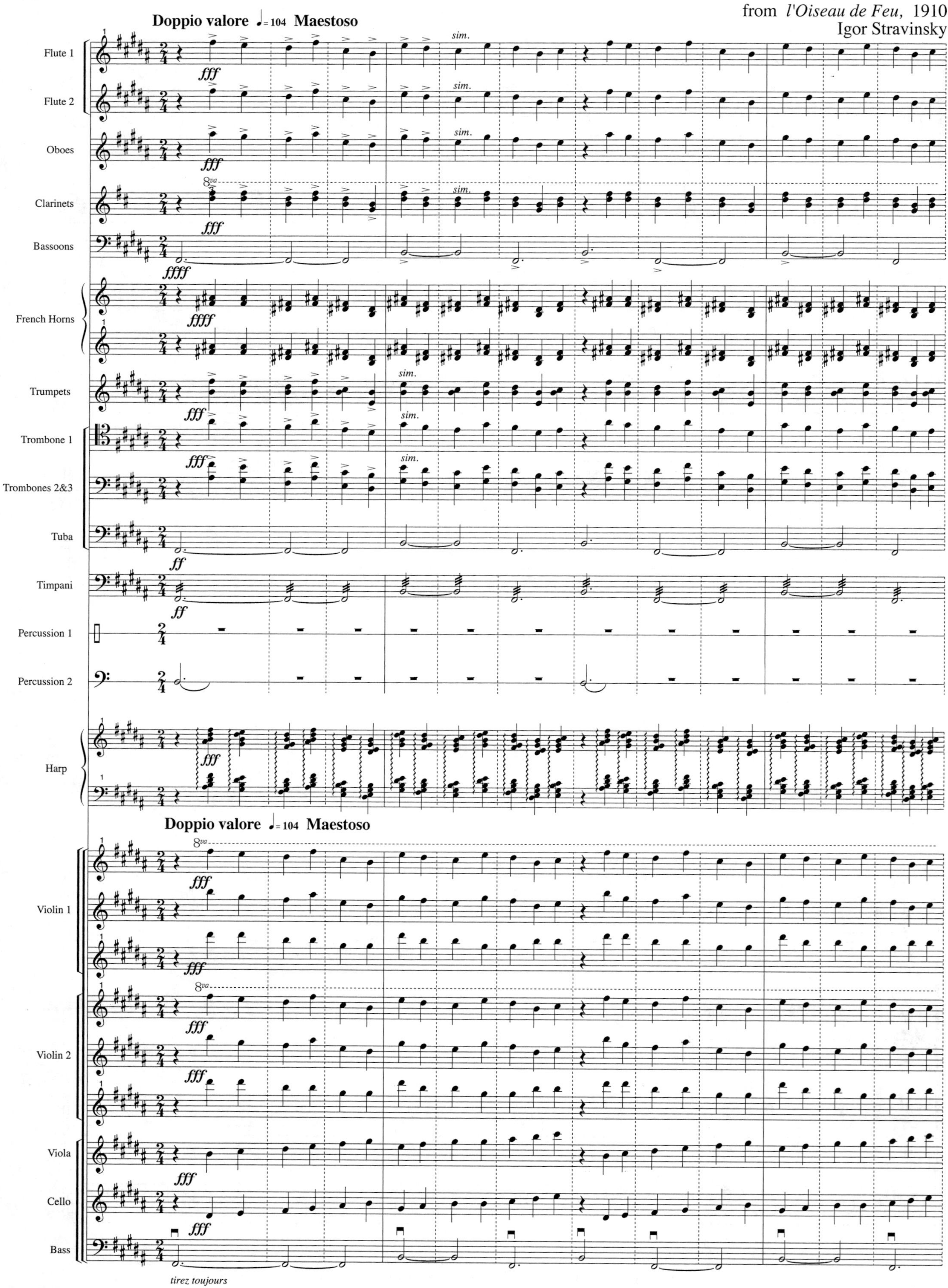

(Score reading #11, cont'd)
Molto pesante ♩= 60
Fl. 1
Fl. 2
Ob.
Cl.
Bsns.
Hns.
Tpts.
Trb. 1
Trbs. 2&3
Tuba
Timp.
Perc. 1
Triangle
Perc. 2
Piatti
Gr.C.
Vln. 1
Vln. 2
Viola
Cello
Bass
sempre più cresc.
sempre più cresc.
ffff
pp subito
sffz
(8va)
tr

from *Elijah*
Felix Mendelssohn

12

from *Gloria*
Antonio Vivaldi

13

String Quartet in D Minor
Franz Schubert

14

Notturno, K. 436
W.A. Mozart
15
5
3
9
Franz Schubert
16

Jesu, Joy of Man's Desiring
J.S. Bach
17
G. Palestrina
18

Class Notes

Scales

All major and minor scales can be divided into 3 "groups" according to their fingering patterns. Each group has its own characteristics and these are listed below. It is recommended that the student memorize each group of scales along with their characteristics and fingerings. Here are some general, introductory statements about scale fingerings.

1. In any scale (major or minor), the 4th finger in each hand only plays ONCE per octave. Consequently, the 4th finger always plays the SAME note. One way to think about scale fingerings is simply to know (memorize) the 4th finger note of each scale.

2. Fingering in scales is CONSECUTIVE, that is -- don't skip fingers. This is a common mistake, particularly skipping the 2nd finger.

Group I Scales: Those scales in which the thumbs always play together.

MAJOR KEYS (thumb notes)   **MINOR KEYS** (thumb notes)

D-Flat	F & C	b-flat	c & f
G-Flat	C-flat & F	e-flat	f & c-flat
B	B & E	b	b & e
F	F & C	f	f & c

Here are some characteristics which may help to play these scales using the correct fingering:

1. The thumbs of each hand always play together. In addition, each scale in this group has 2 thumb notes (see the above chart). The thumbs always play on the white notes — never on black notes.

2. For all the scales in this group, the 2nd and 3rd fingers of each hand play on or near the group of 2 black notes. The 2nd, 3rd, & 4th fingers of each hand play on or near the group of 3 black notes.

Group II Scales: Those scales which have the same fingering as C major.

Major: C D E G A
Minor: c d e g a

All four forms of the scales in Group 2 have the same fingering: major, natural minor, harmonic minor, and melodic minor. Listed below are some characteristics of Group 2 scales which may help you to play the scales using the correct fingering:

1. All scales in Group 2 have the same fingering as C Major:

RH: 1, 2, 3, 1, 2, 3, 4, 1, 2, 3, 1, 2, 3, 4, 5
LH: 5, 4, 3, 2, 1, 3, 2, 1, 4, 3, 2, 1, 3, 2, 1

2. 3rd fingers in each hand play together.
3. Right hand 4th finger plays only the 7th degree of the scale.
4. Left hand 4th finger plays only the 2nd degree of the scale.
5. The thumbs play together only on the tonic note.

Group I Scales

All scales should be played from memory, 2 octaves ascending and descending in a steady tempo with correct fingering.

D♭ Major
(Thumb notes: f & c)

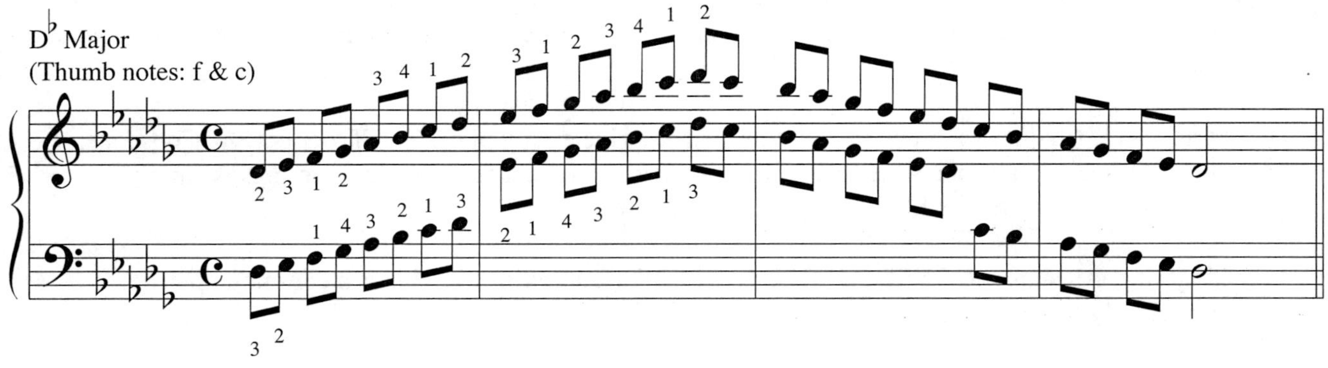

G♭ Major
(Thumb notes: c♭ & f)

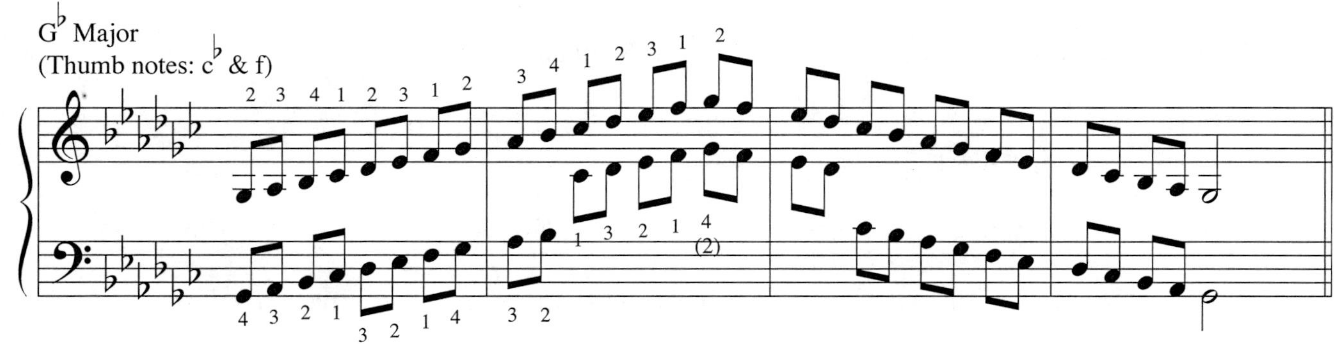

B Major
(Thumb notes: b & e)

F Major
(Thumb notes: f & c)

Group I Scales, cont'd

Group I Scales, cont'd

Group II Scales

Group II Scales, cont'd

Group II Scales, cont'd

Group II Scales, cont'd

Group I Arpeggios

All arpeggios should be played from memory, 2 octaves ascending and descending in a steady tempo with correct fingering. Unlike scales, there are several sets of fingering which different teachers use to teach arpeggios. You should use the fingering your instructor recommends. However, below is outlined a commonly used set of arpeggio fingering.

As with scales, arpeggios can be grouped according to specific fingering patterns. However, the groups of scales and arpeggios are not the same event thought there are coincidently three groups of arpeggio fingering.

GROUP I (fingered like C Major):   Right hand: 1 2 3 1 2 3 5
                                        Left hand: 5 4 2 1 4 2 1

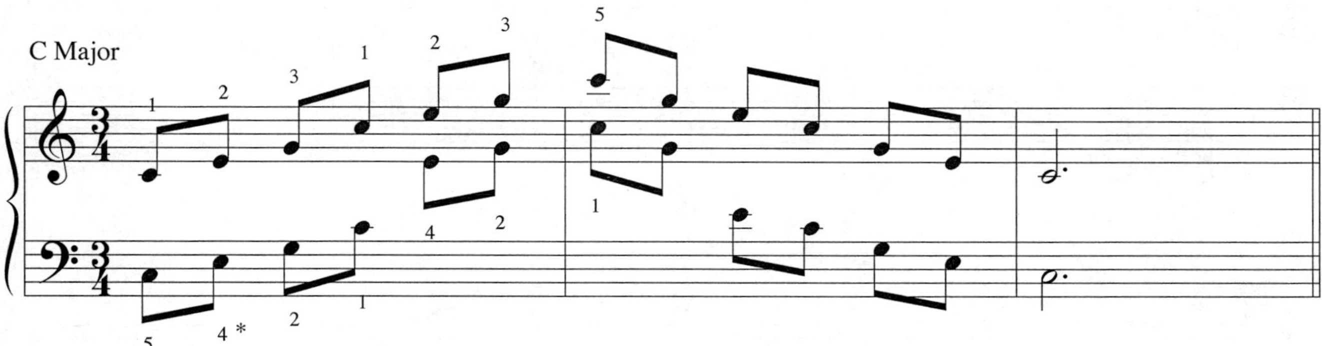

* Be sure to use the 4th finger in the left hand.

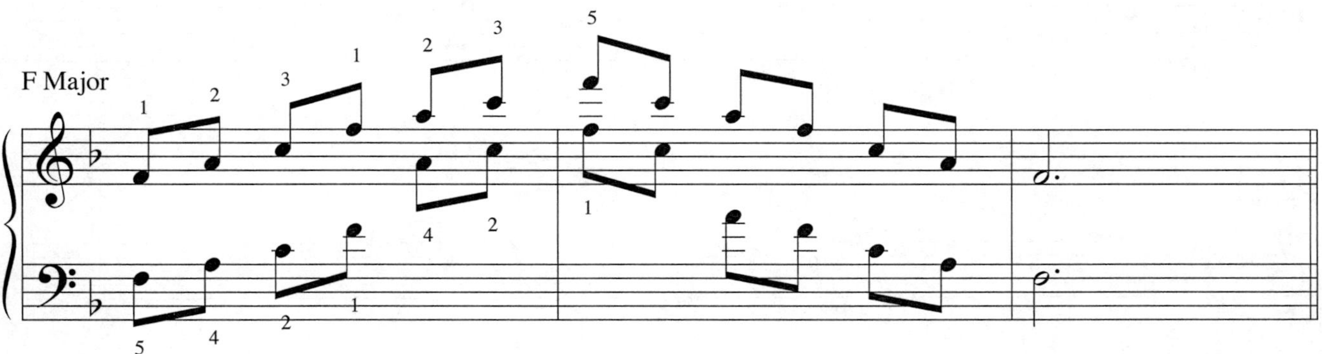

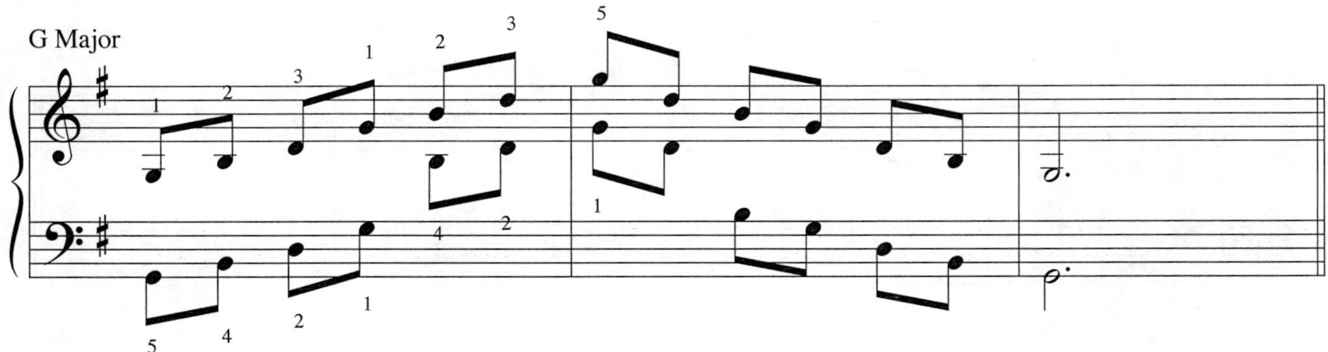

Group I Arpeggios, cont'd

Group I Arpeggios, cont'd

Group II Arpeggios

Group II arpeggios have the same fingering as Group I, except use of the 3rd finger in the left hand instead of the 4th.

Scale and Arpeggio Practice Log

Scales	1	2	3	4	5	6	7	8	9	10	11	12	13	14	15	16	17	18	19
D-flat																			
G-flat																			
B																			
F																			
B-flat minor																			
E-flat minor																			
B minor																			
F minor																			
C																			
D																			
E																			
G																			
A																			
C minor																			
D minor																			
E minor																			
G minor																			
A minor																			

Arpeggios	1	2	3	4	5	6	7	8	9	10	11	12	13	14	15	16	17	18	19
C																			
F																			
G																			
C minor																			
D minor																			
E minor																			
F minor																			
G minor																			
A minor																			
B minor																			
E-flat minor																			
D																			
E																			
A																			
B																			
G-flat																			

Exercises

Exercise #1 Ascending

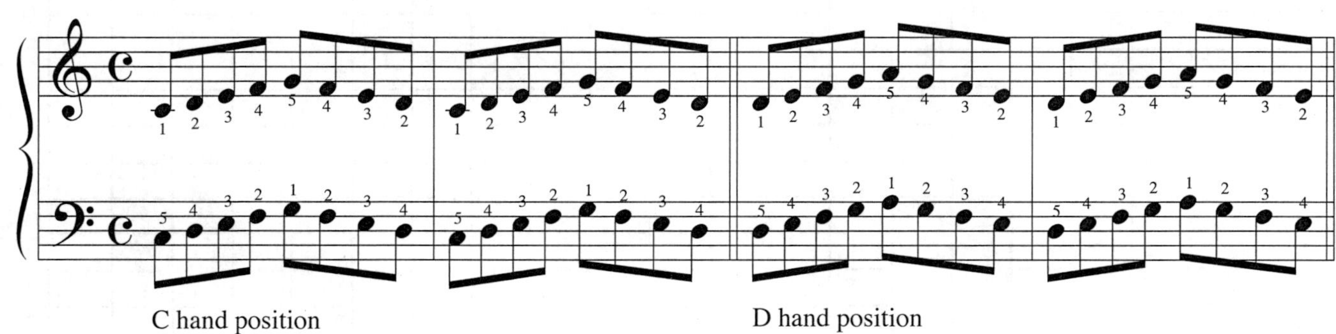

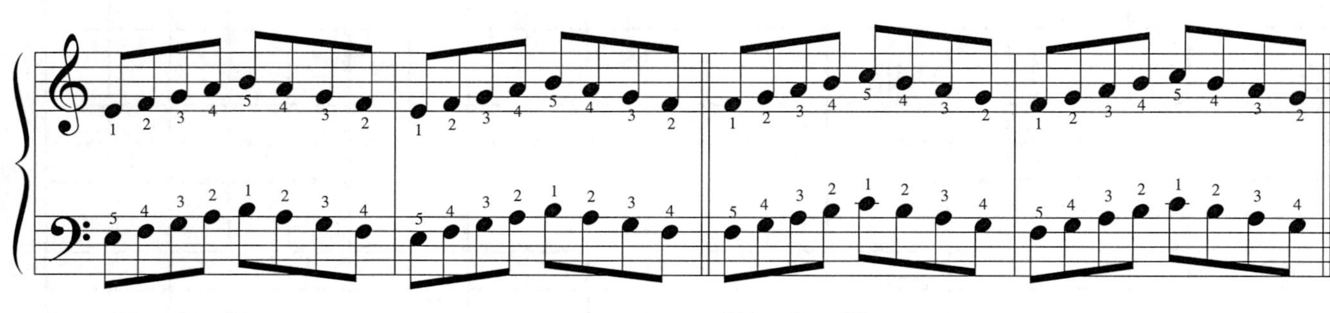

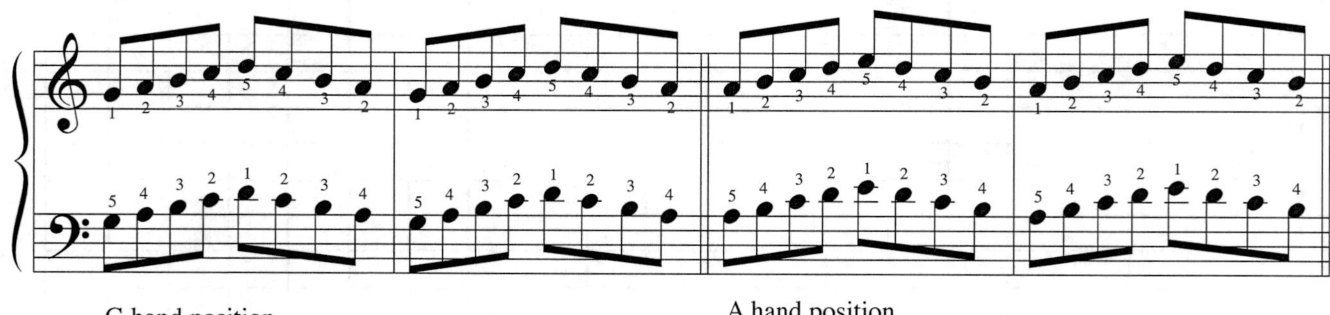

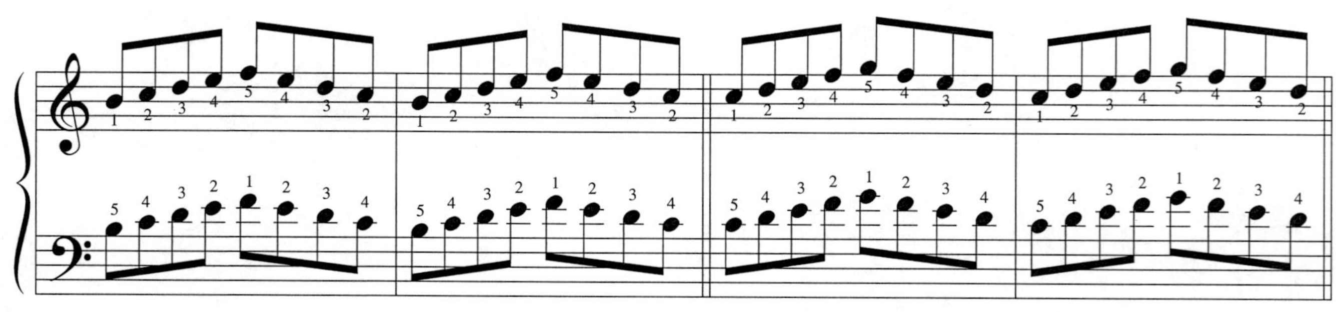

Exercise #1 Descending

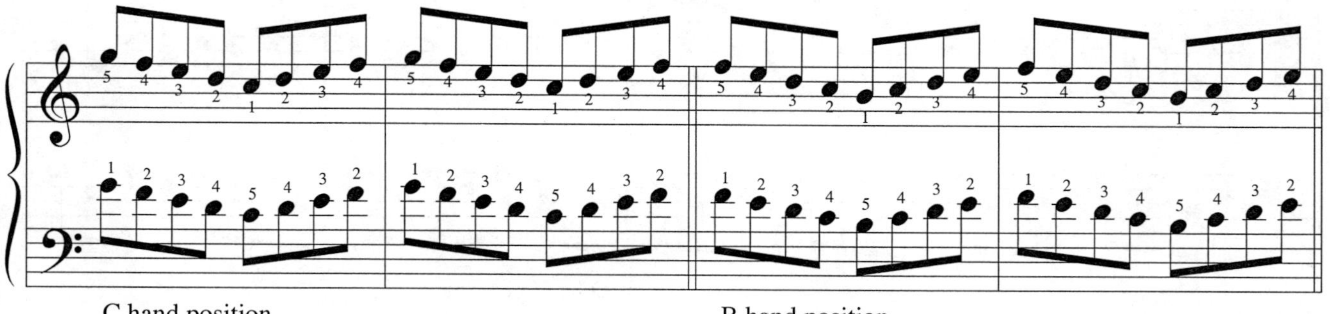

C hand position   B hand position

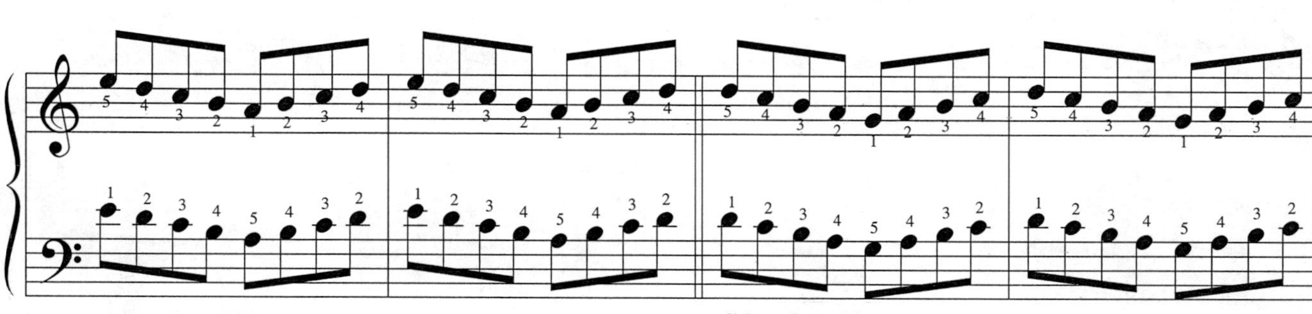

A hand position   G hand position

F hand position   E hand position

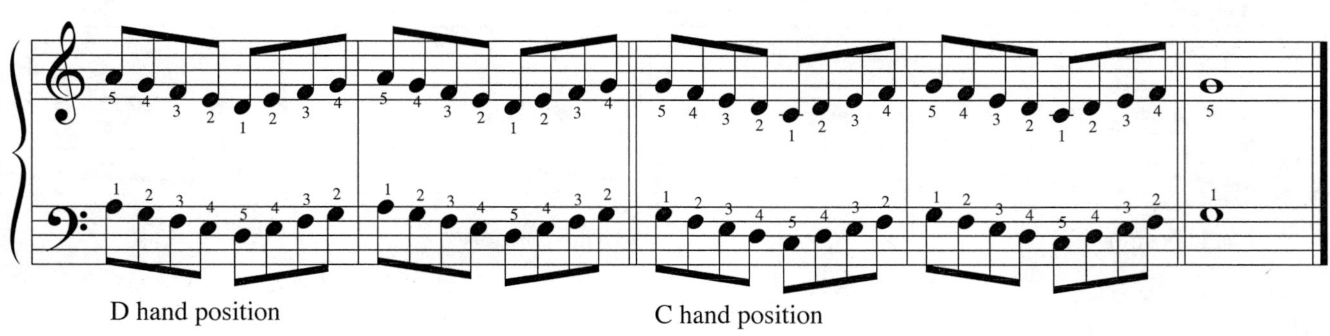

D hand position   C hand position

Exercise #2 Ascending

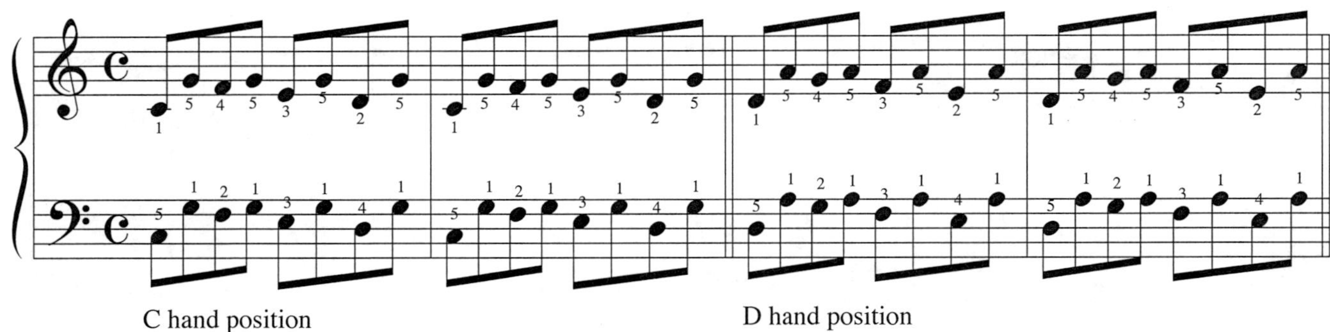

C hand position
D hand position

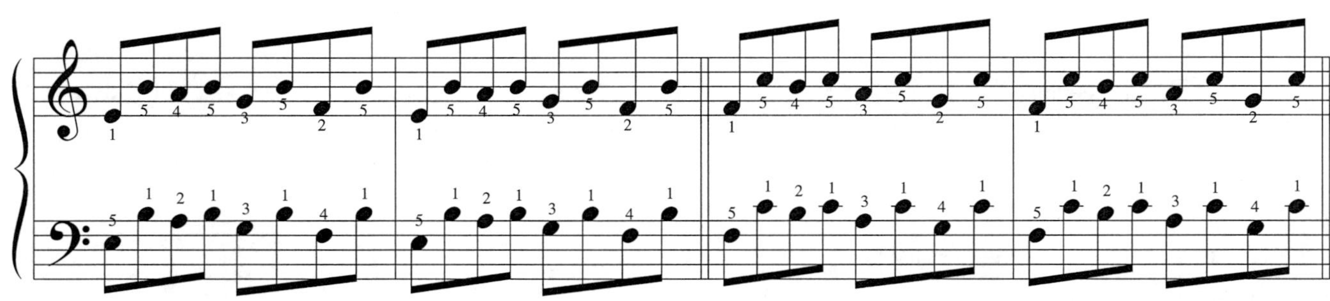

E hand position
F hand position

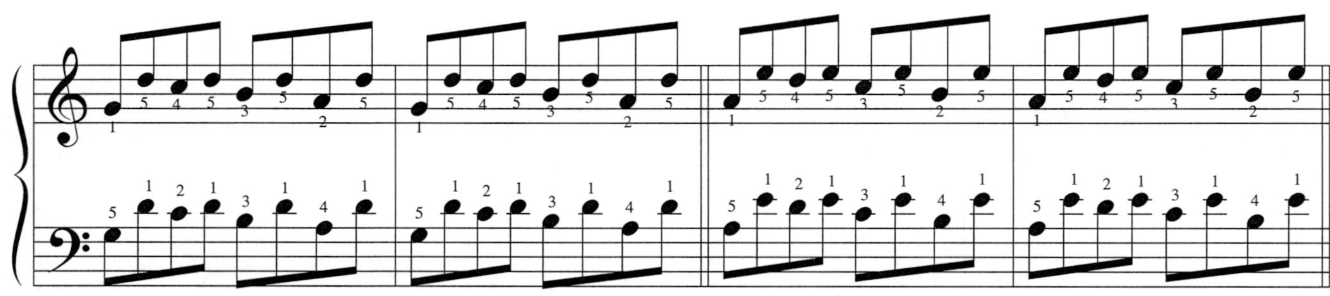

G hand position
A hand position

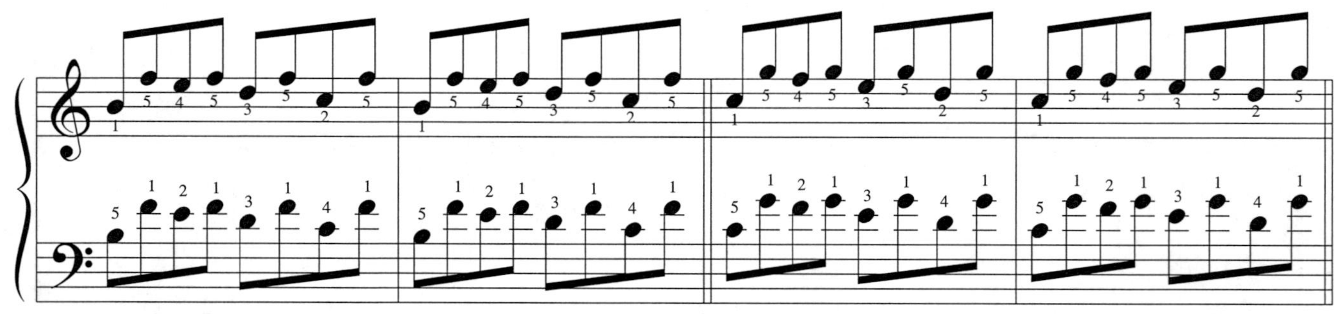

B hand position
C hand position

Exercise #2 Descending

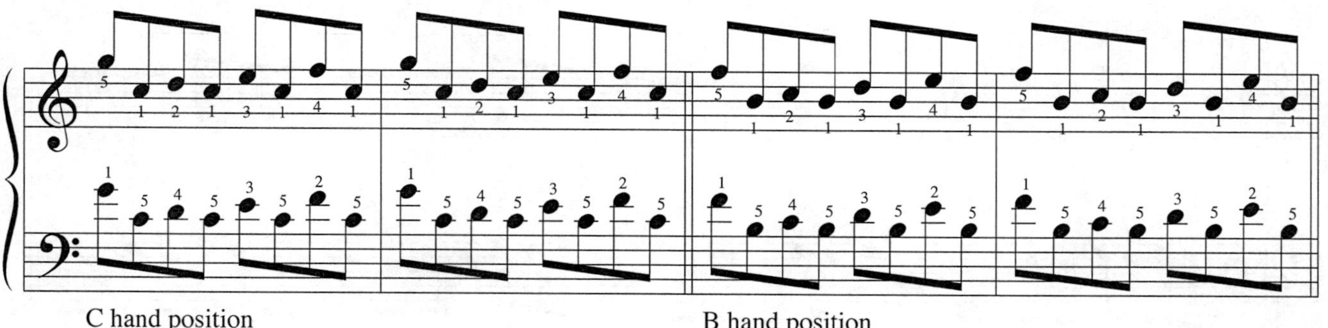

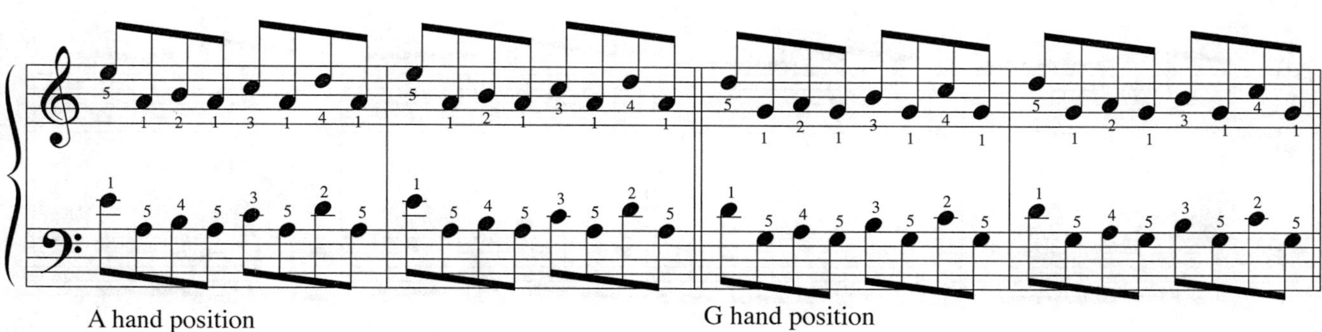

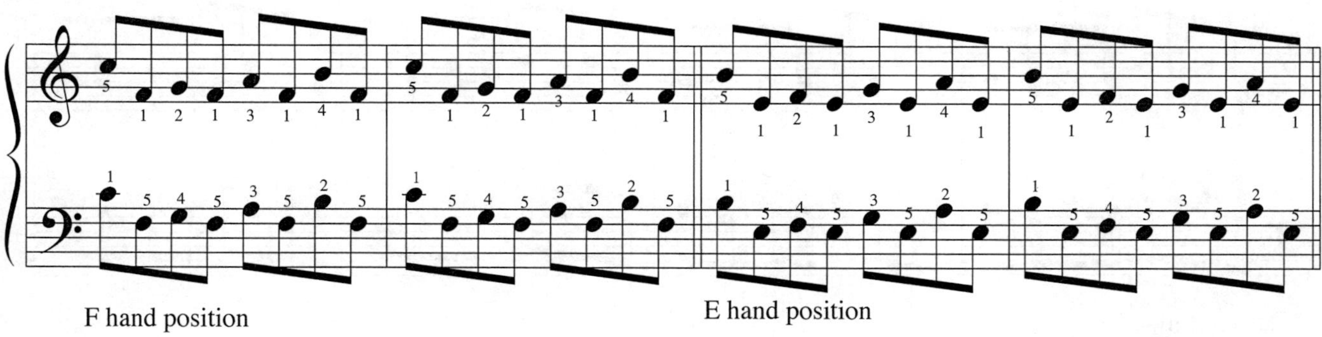

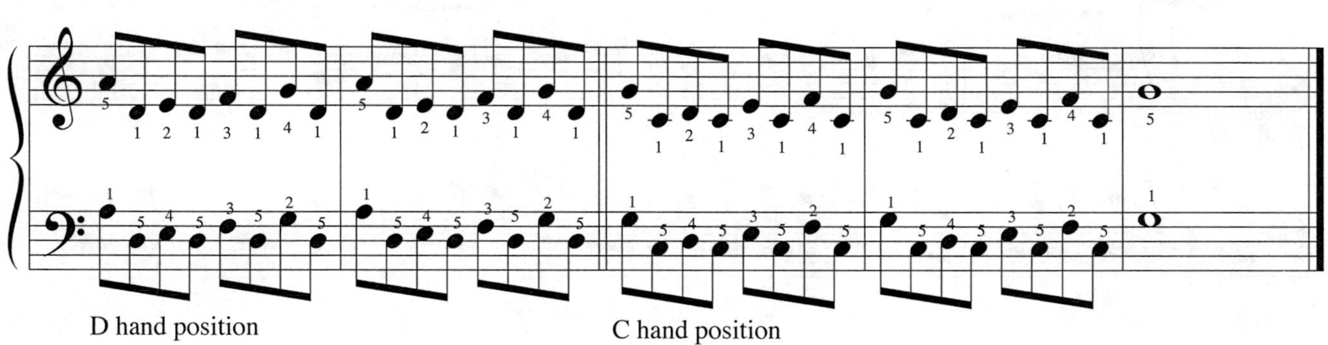

Exercise #3 Ascending

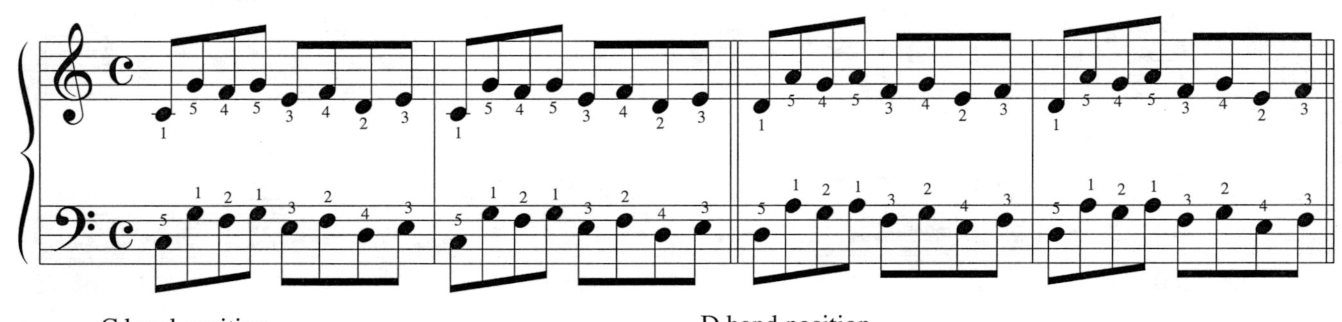

C hand position   D hand position

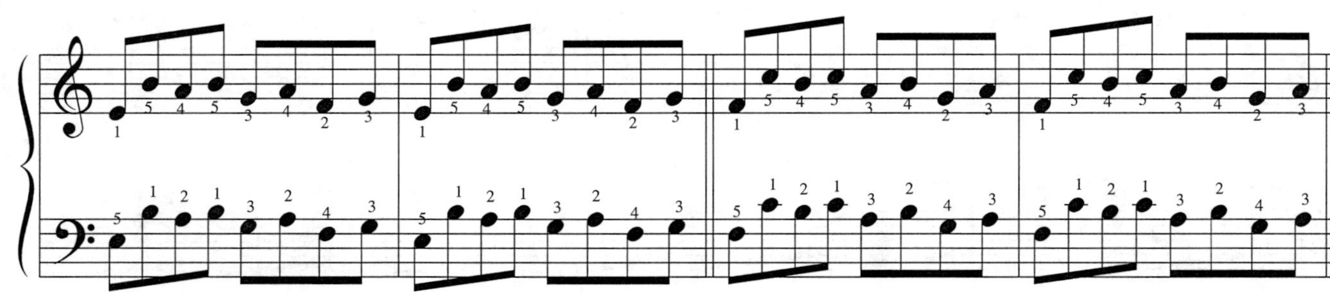

E hand position   F hand position

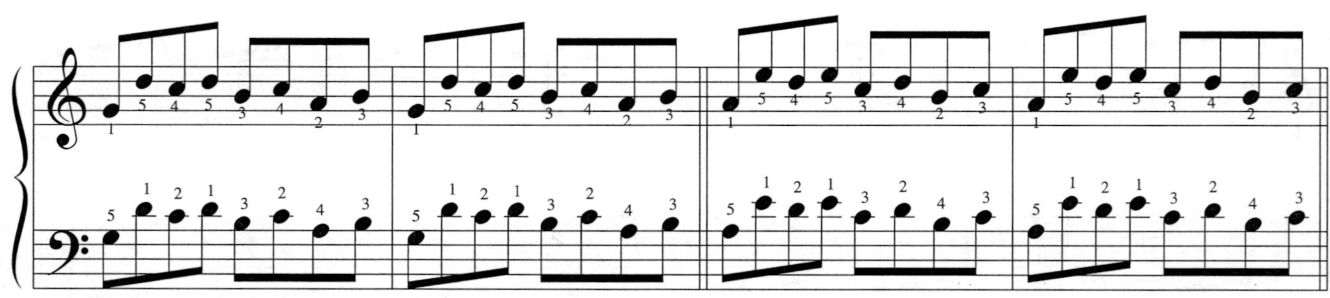

G hand position   A hand position

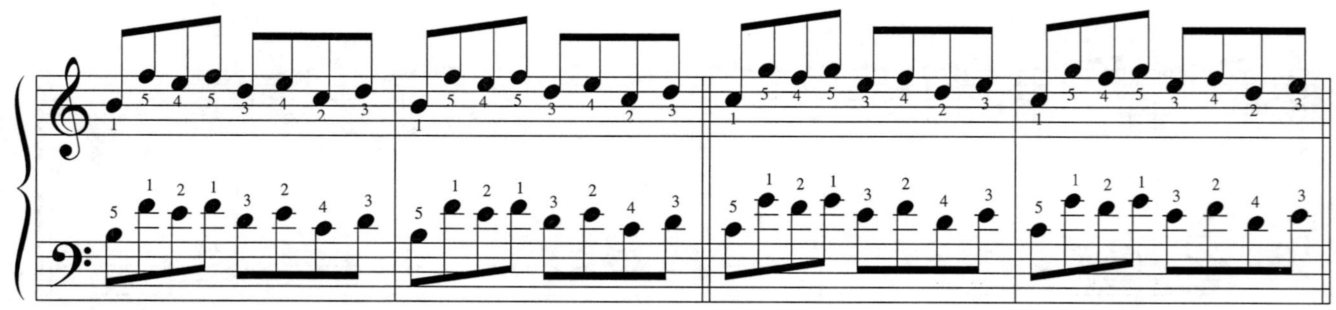

B hand position   C hand position

Exercise #3 Descending

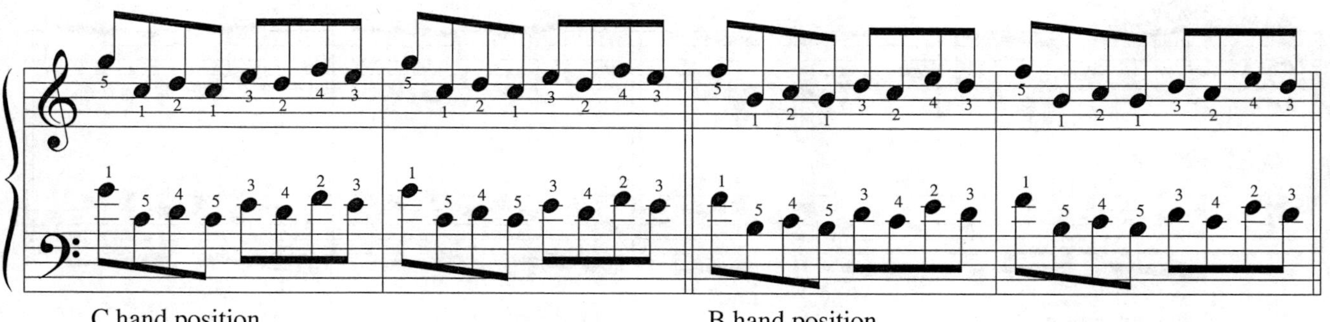

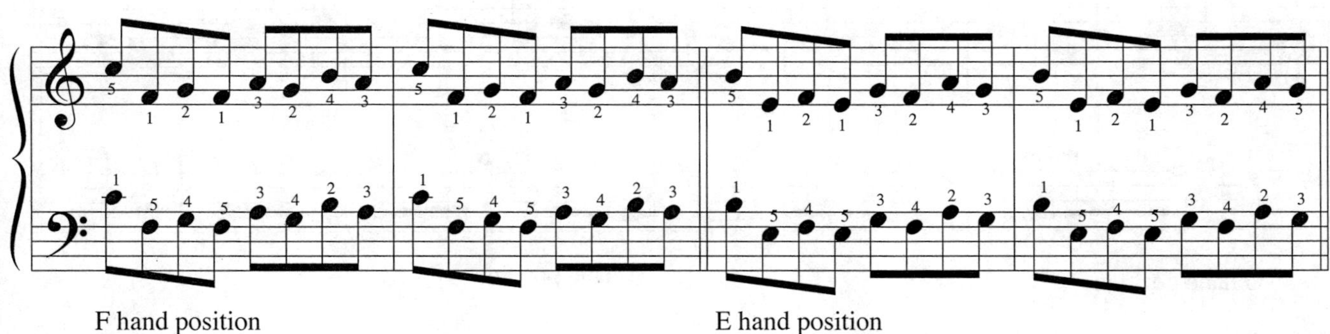

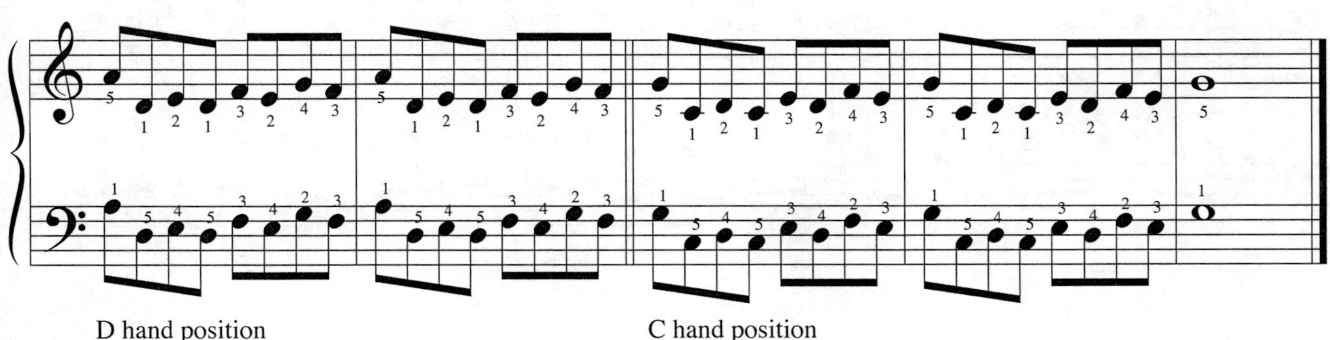

110

Exercise #4 Ascending

C hand position

D hand position

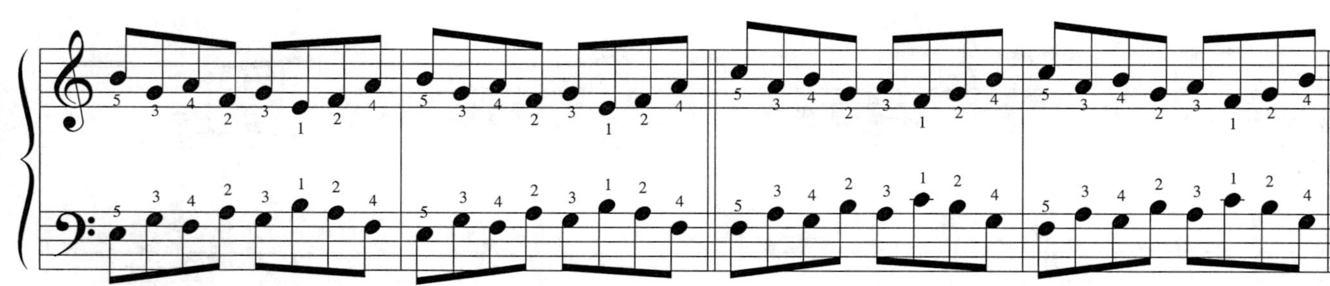

E hand position

F hand position

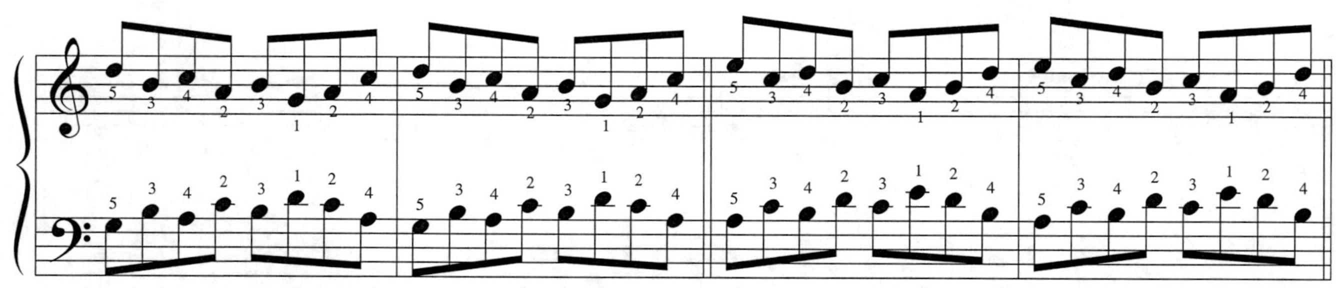

G hand position

A hand position

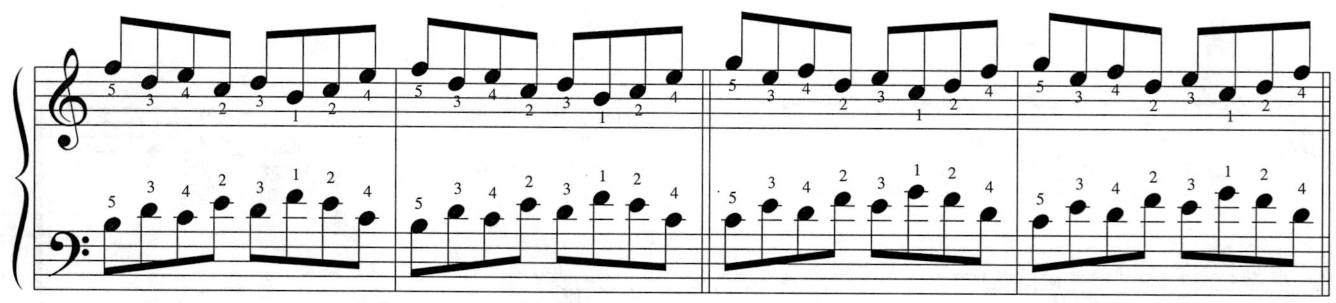

B hand position

C hand position

Exercise #4 Descending

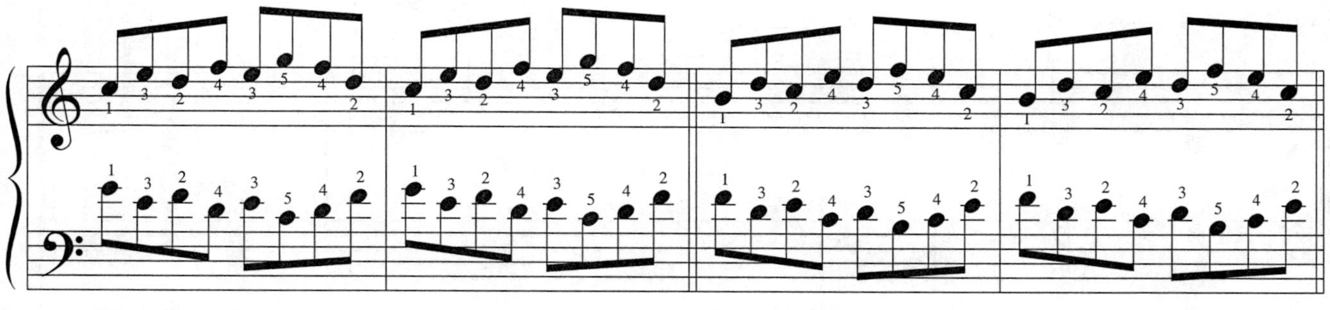

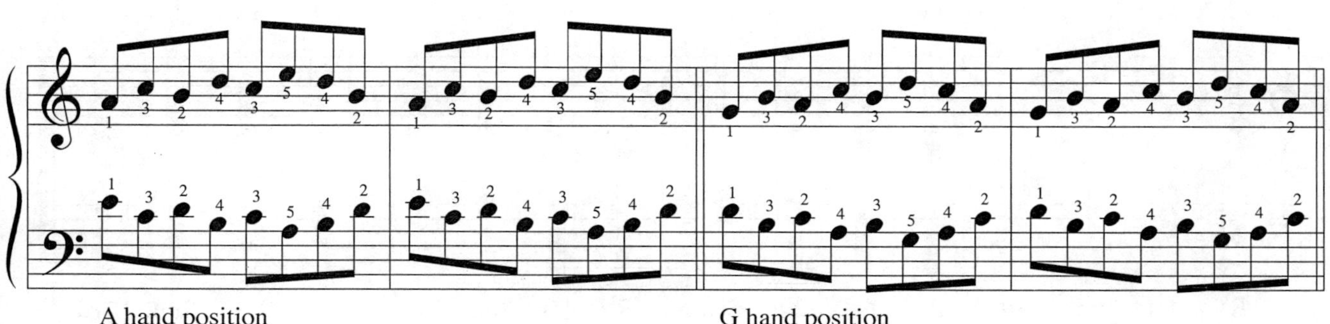

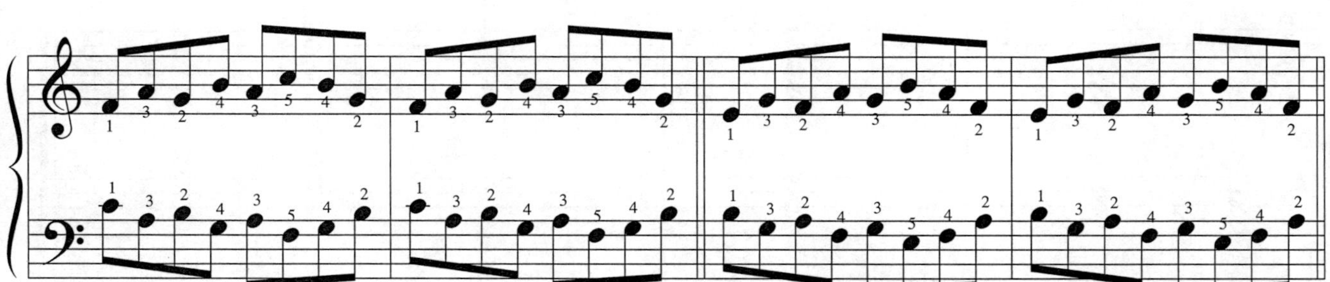

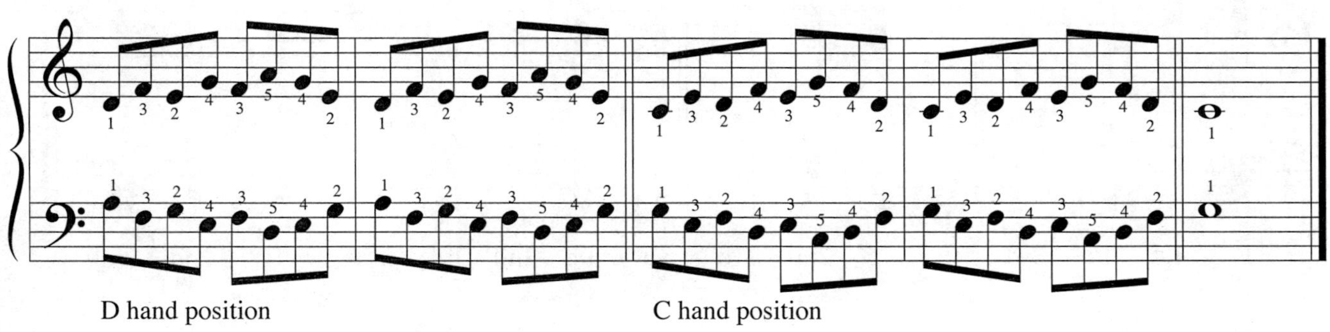

Appendix 1: Triads in a Scale; Inversions of Triads

Root position triads: C Major

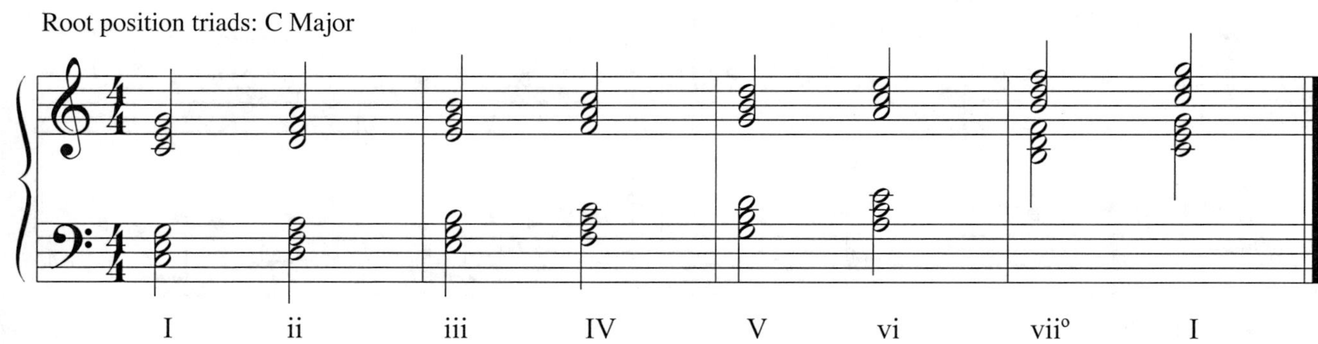

Inversions of primary triads: C Major

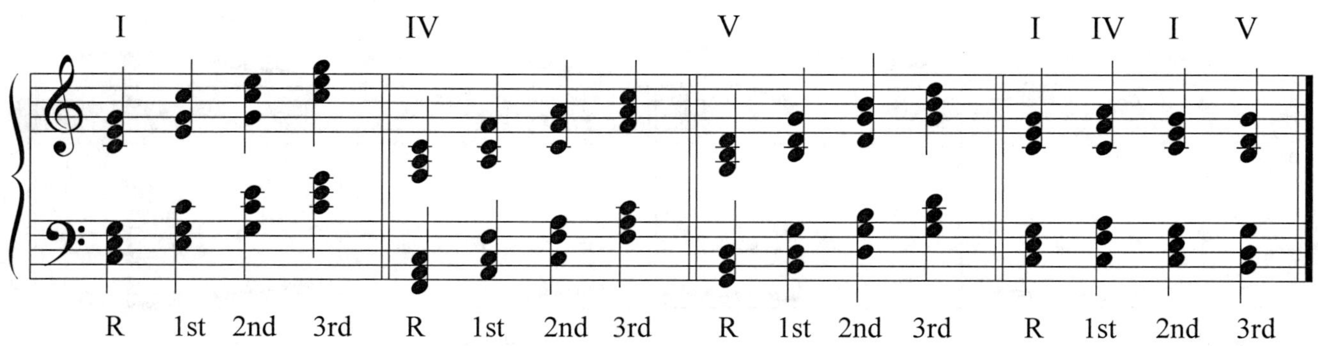

Root position triads: A minor

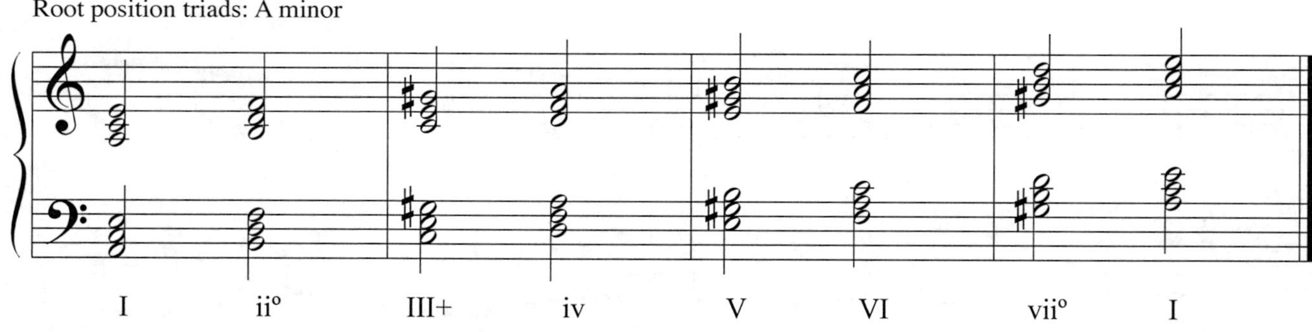

Inversions of primary triads: A minor

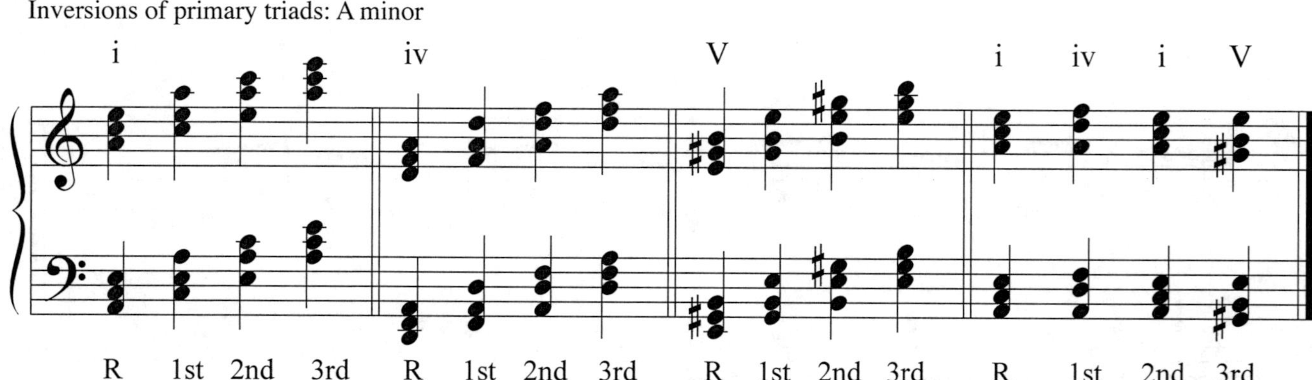

Appendix 1: Triads/inversions cont'd

Root position triads: F Major

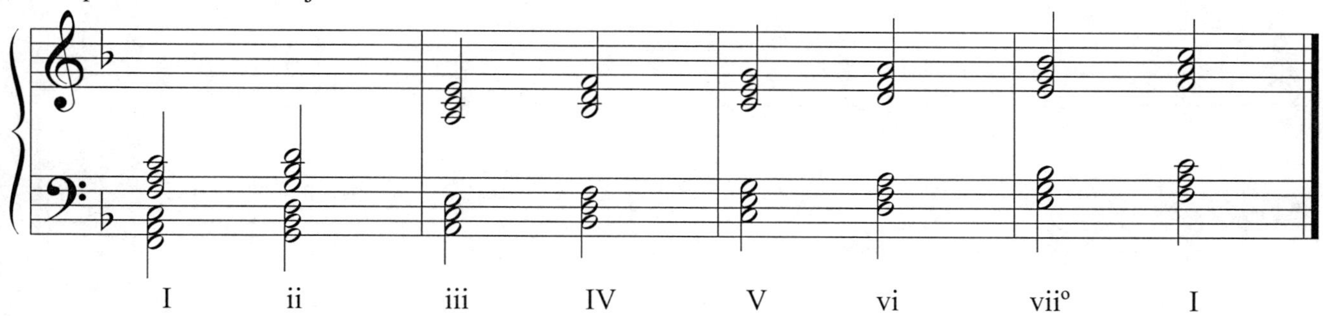

Inversions of primary triads: F Major

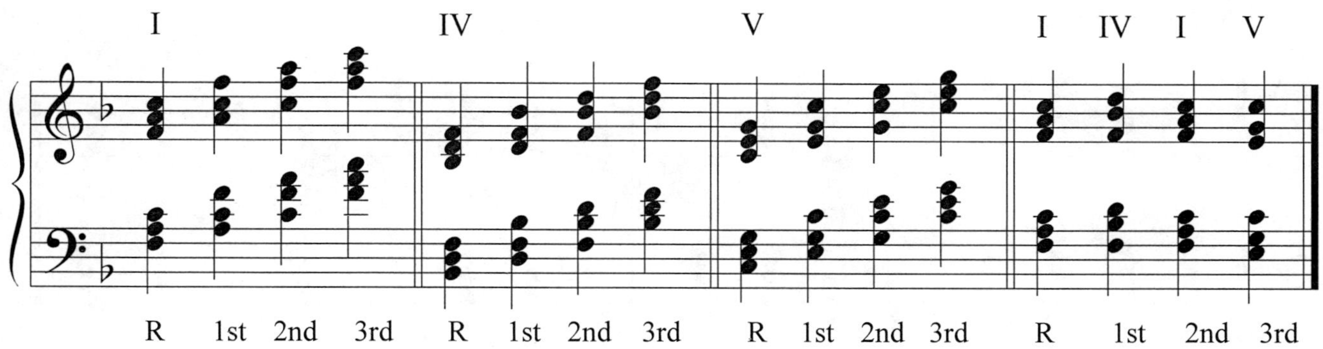

Root position triads: D minor

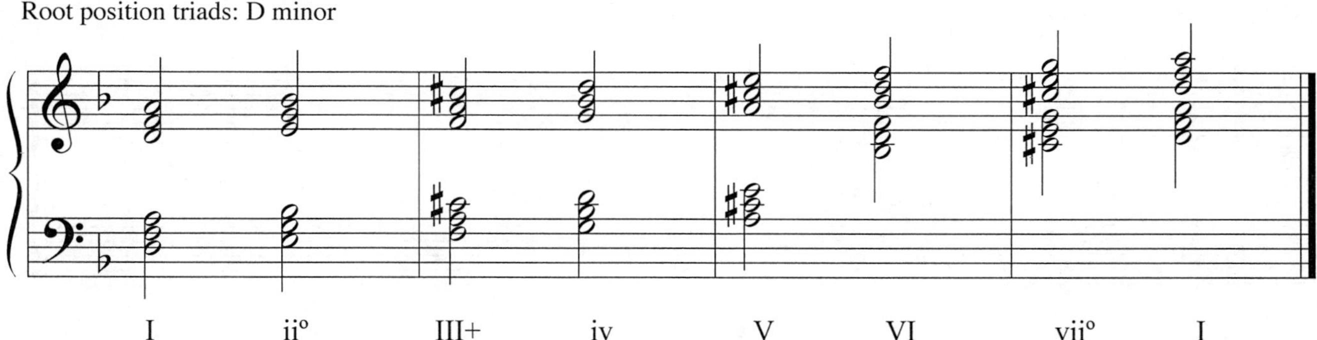

Inversions of primary triads: D minor

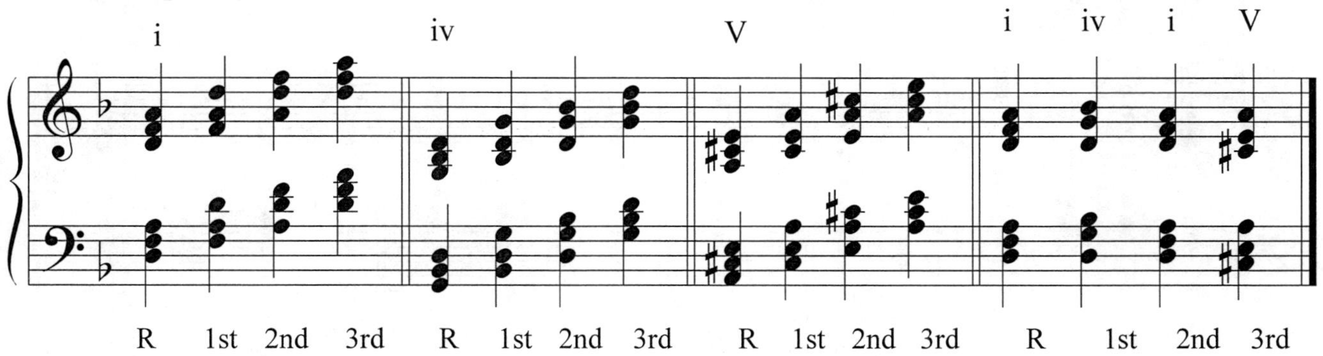

Appendix 1: Triads/inversions cont'd

Root position triads: G Major

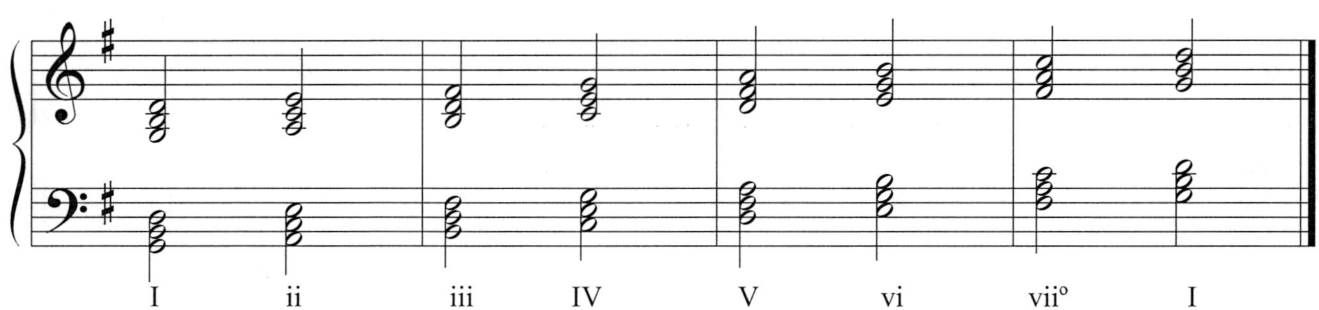

Inversions of primary triads: G Major

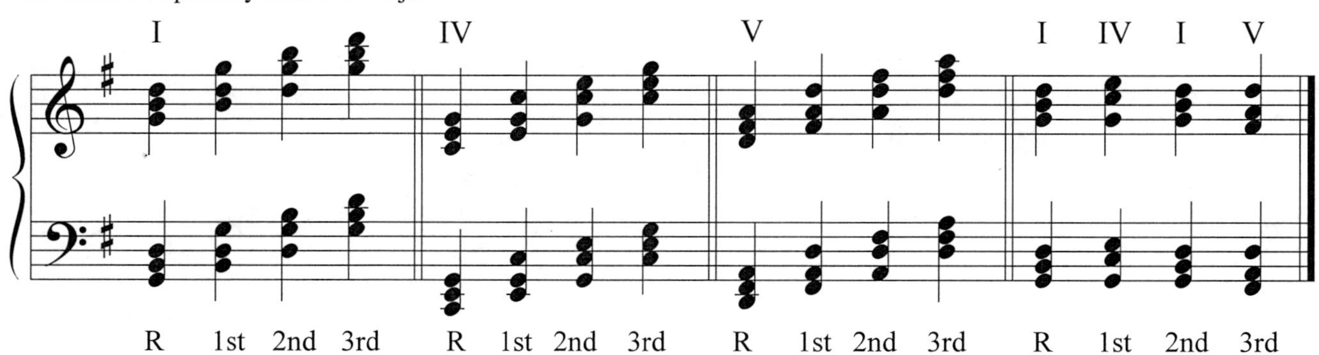

Root position triads: E minor

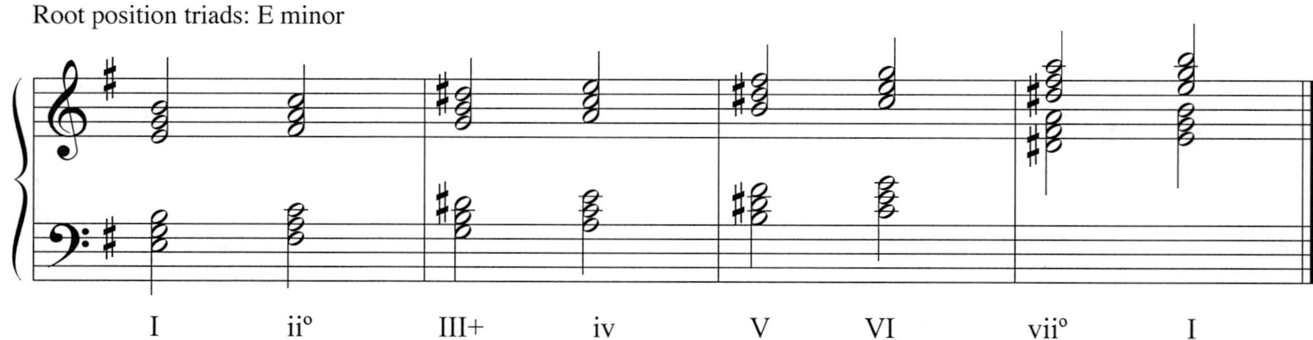

Inversions of primary triads: E minor

Appendix 1: Triads/inversions cont'd

Root position triads: D Major

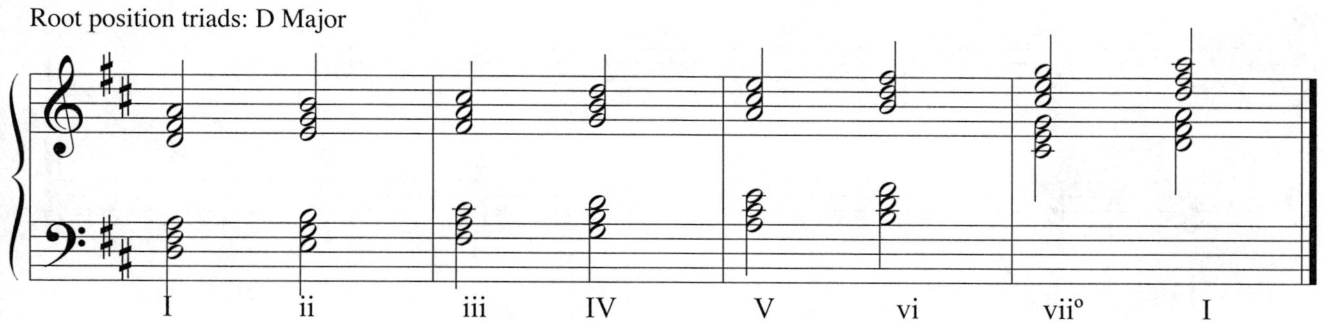

Inversions of primary triads: D Major

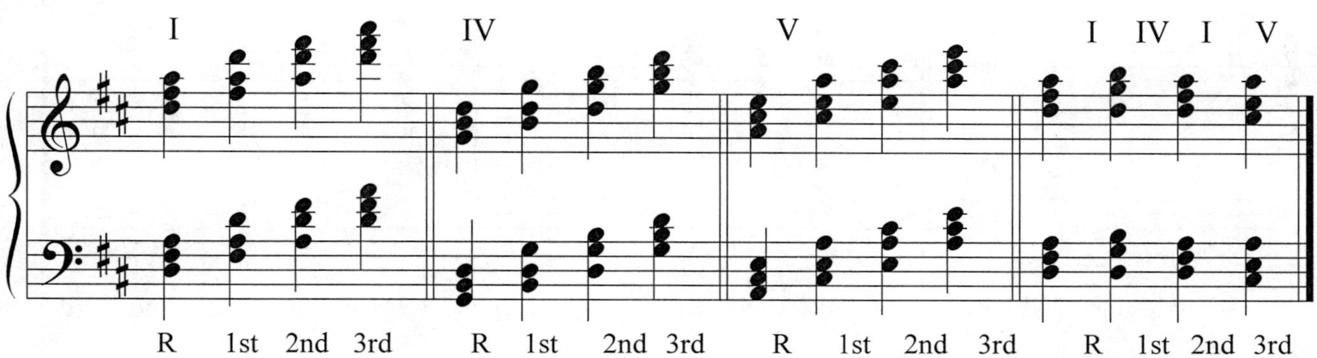

Root position triads: B minor

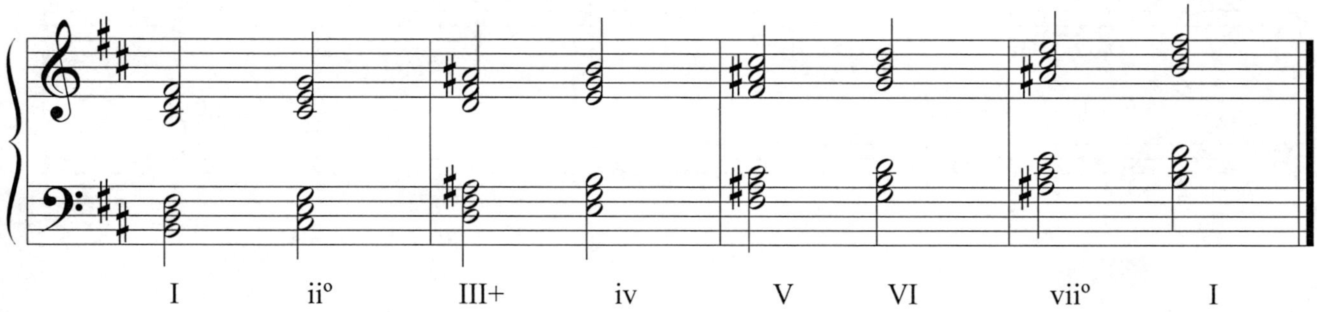

Inversions of primary triads: B minor

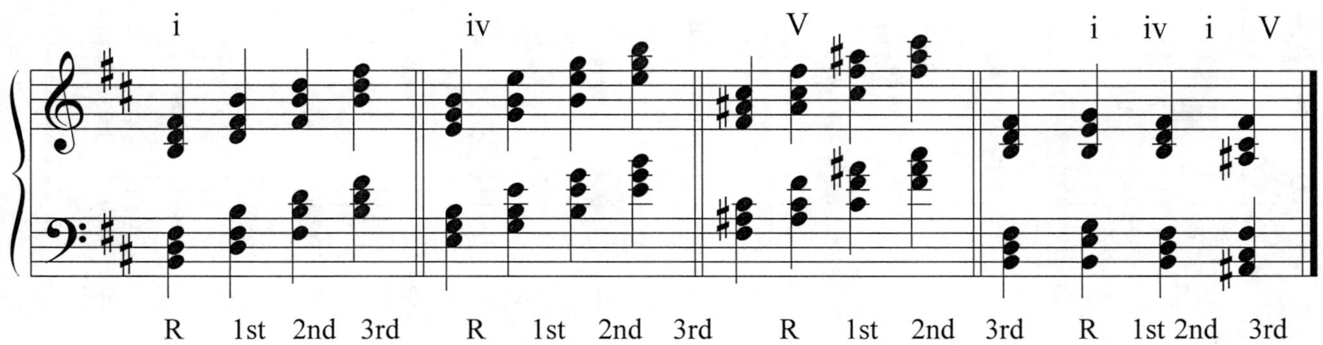

Appendix 1: Triads/inversions cont'd

Root position triads: B♭ Major

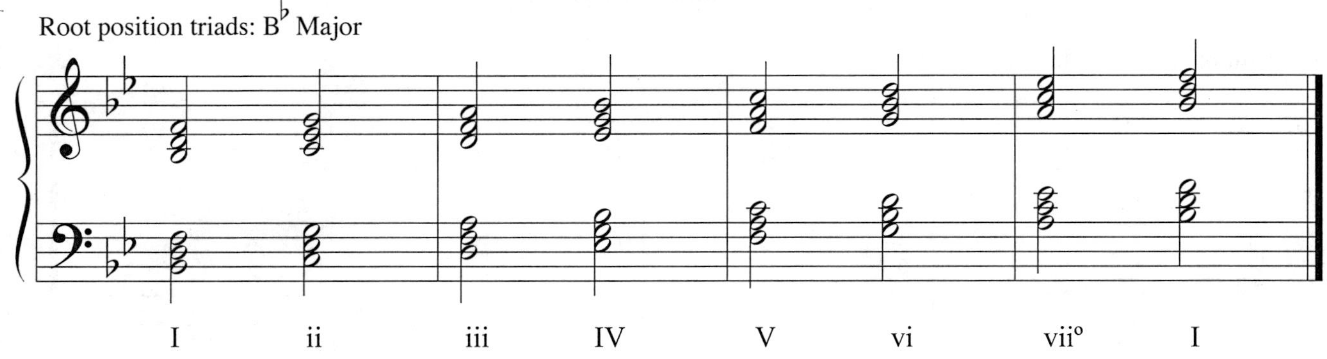

Inversions of primary triads: B♭ Major

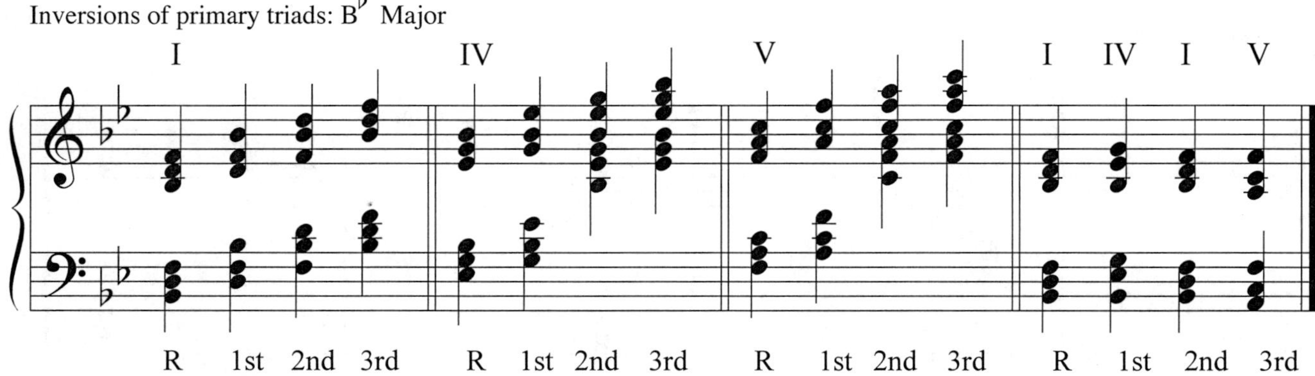

Root position triads: G minor

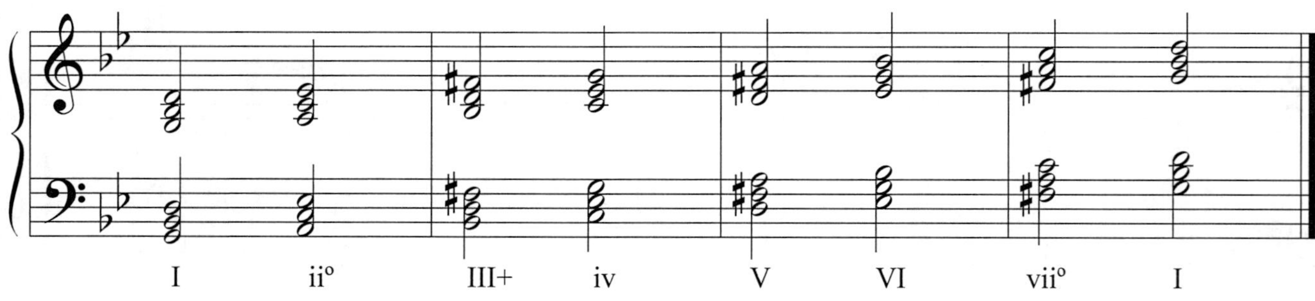

Inversions of primary triads: g harmonic minor

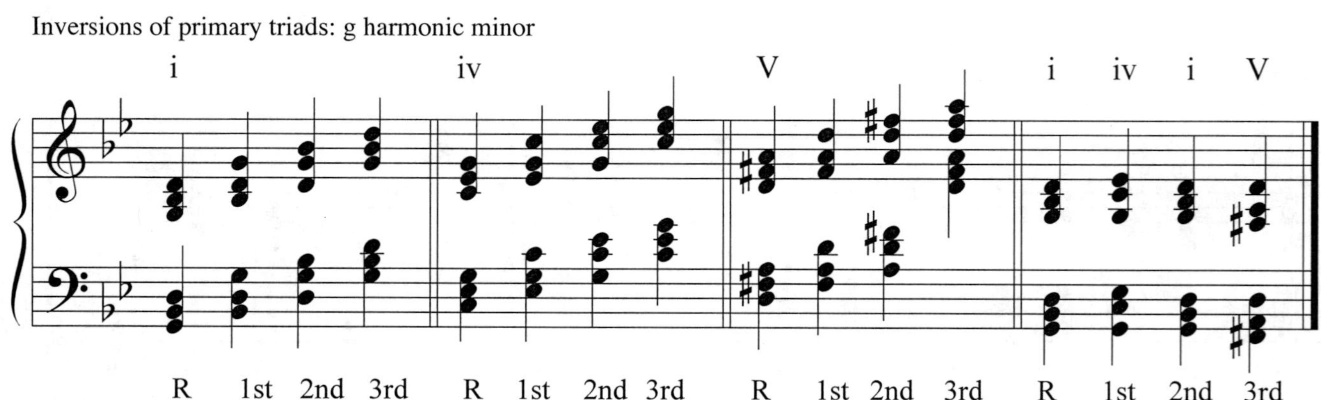

Appendix 2: Melodic Phrases

The material presented here is intended to supplement the harmonized melody and improvisation examples. "Melodic phrase" refers to the phrase construction found in simple common melodies such as popular music, folk tunes, hymn tunes and chorales. Although this material may apply to phrase construction found in larger classical music literature, generally the melodic phrase construction of art music is more complex and is beyond the scope of these materials.

Melodies are comprised of PHRASES. For example, the following melody consists of three phrases:

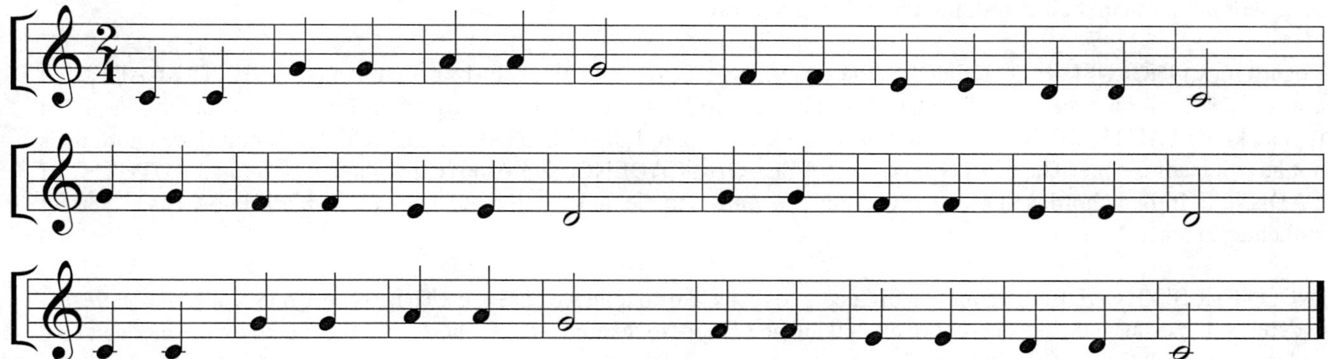

Here is a common definition of PHRASE:

> A phrase is the SHORTest passage of music expressing a COMPLETE MUSICAL THOUGHT and ending in a CADENCE.*

There are three key points to this definition: (1) short, (2) complete musical thought, and (3) cadence. Hopefully, "short" will not need extensive elaboration. However, a common error in determining a phrase is getting it TOO short. More on this later.

COMPLETE MUSICAL THOUGHT means an instance of tension / relaxation. This duality is the basis of "complete musical thought" and is related to the same kind of duality present in classical poetic meters. In the above example, each phrase can easily be divided into its respective tension / relaxation (i.e., each phrase = 4 meas.; tension = 2 meas., relaxation = 2 meas.; half notes indicate points of division).   Not all melodies are this obvious. However, a great number of successful melodies do consist of combinations of 4 or 8 measure phrases. With this explanation of "complete musical thought" in mind, examine the above melody again. It is easy to understand why some might make the mistake of defining the phrases in this melody as consisting of 2 measures instead of 4 measures. However, after playing or singing this example the tension / relaxation scenario should become apparent. This particular melody has three phrases and in that regard is not as common as many melodies which have 2 or 4 phrases.

In the above definition, "cadence" does not mean what it meant in an earlier section of this book -- a simple progression of block chords. Instead, CADENCE here means a point of relaxation of the tension at the end of the phrase. There are specific kinds of cadences and all phrases end with one of these specific cadences (see Appendix 3).

Analyze the melodies in the **Melodies for Harmonization** section of this book to determine their phrase construction. In addition to finding tension / relaxation, you might look for these often obvious characteristics of phrase construction:

- •. Sometimes the CADENCE POINT is the longest note value of the phrase. See examples #7, p. 40; #37, p. 47.

- • Often phrases consist of 4 or 8 measures (depending on the tempo), as in the example above.

* Definition based on Douglass Green's, *Form in Tonal Music*, 3rd edition, Harcourt Brace Jovanovich College Publisher, 1979.

Appendix 3: Melodic Cadences

As mentioned in **Appendix 2**, melodic phrases end with a cadence. In this sense, "cadence" refers to what happens at the end of a phrase and has nothing to do with the "block-chord" cadences (chord progressions) that you are required to learn in order to harmonize melodies and improvise. Here, CADENCE is a "point of rest" at the end of a phrase.

There are only TWO categories of cadences: (1) conclusive, and (2) inconclusive. All types of cadences fall into these two categories. A CONCLUSIVE CADENCE is a cadence on the I chord and an INCONCLUSIVE CADENCE is a cadence on a chord other than the I chord, for example the V chord.

Regarding CONCLUSIVE CADENCES, there are 2 types: (a) authentic, and (b) plagal. An AUTHENTIC CADENCE consists of 2 chords where the PENULTIMATE (next-to-last) chord contains a leading tone. Consequently, the most typical kind of AUTHENTIC CADENCE is V or V7 moving to I. In a PLAGAL CADENCE, the penultimate chord does not have a leading tone. The most typical kind of PLAGAL CADENCE is IV moving to the I chord. In an AUTHENTIC CADENCE, if the I chord is in root position and the tonic is in the melody (top most voice), then it is known as a "perfect authentic cadence."

INCONCLUSIVE CADENCES are not divided into types like conclusive cadences. There is only one type of inconclusive cadence -- those that cadence on a chord other than the I chord, for example the V chord. Another name for the inconclusive cadence is HALF CADENCE. It is important to know that a cadence on V is not the definition of "half cadence" but merely an EXAMPLE of a half cadence. Other half cadences could be cadences on IV ("Auld Lang Syne"), cadences on III ("I've been working on the rail road"), and cadences on vi (deceptive cadence). There is no such thing as a "perfect half cadence." PERFECT when applied to a cadence only refers to an authentic cadence.

To successfully harmonize a melody, it is important to have a step-by-step procedure rather than just willy-nilly sticking in chords. Here is a practical procedure for harmonizing a melody. If you use this you will have consistent success:

    1. Identify the phrases. Often phrases can be identified by counting 4 or 8 measures (the majority of common melodies in the western tradition have phrases constructed of 4 or 8 measures), looking for the longest note value (often the cadence point at the end of a phrase is the longest note value of the phrase), or by looking for some aspect of tension and relaxation (question/answer). See the melody below for reference.

    2. Harmonize the CADENCE POINTS first. The cadence point is the 2nd chord of the two-chord progression of the cadence, for example V7 - I. The V7 chord is the "penultimate chord" and the I chord is the "cadence point." Generally, there are only two possibilities to harmonize the cadence point: I or V. Remember (from above), there are ONLY TWO categories of cadences: conclusive and non conclusive. So, once you identify the cadence points at the ends of the various phrases it should be relatively easy to determine if the cadence points are I or V. If the cadence point is a V, then it is better to cadence on V rather than V7 (although for Level I piano, the V chord voicing is not presented so it is OK to cadence on V7 rather than V).

    3. Next, harmonize the PENULTIMATE CHORD -- that is, the chord right before the cadence point. If the cadence point is the I chord, then you have two possibilities: (a) V7 - I, or (b) IV - I. In the first case that would be an authentic cadence and in the second case it would be a plagal cadence. It most cases it simply doesn't matter which possibility you use. If the cadence point is not a I chord (it's going to be an inconclusive cadence), then your 1st choice should be the V chord since BY FAR this is the most common inconclusive (half) cadence. Yes, there are rare example where a IV chord or a III chord would work, but your BEST CHOICE would simply be to use the V chord. Do not cadence on a ii chord. If you feel the chord HAS to be the ii chord, then chances are you are trying to harmonize the "tension" part of the phrase (as in, tension/relaxation) and you have not really found the true cadence point of the phrase.

    4. Harmonize the rest of the melody. Now that you have the cadences at the ends of the phrases harmonized, go ahead and harmonize the rest of the melody using the suggested harmonic rhythm. From here on out, the harmonization procedure will be relative straight forward: if the melody note is in the chord you are trying to use, then IT WILL WORK. There are some simple guidelines to use: (a) often the melody notes will outline specific chords and this will be a good

Material based on Douglass Green's, *Form in Tonal Music*, 3rd edition, Harcourt Brace Jovanovich College Publisher, 1979.

clue as to what chord to use, (b) it's OK to use the same chord consecutively -- you don't have to change chords on every instances of the harmonic rhythm, (c) V7-I used within the phrase works best when the I chord is on a strong beat and the V7 chord is on a weak beat. This is not a hard and fast rule, but it generally works well.

Here is an example:

Find the phrases, identify and then harmonize the cadence points. How many phrases does this tune have?

-- The answer is TWO PHRASES. Count 8 measure phrases and look for the LONGEST note values.
-- The longest note values ARE the CADENCE POINTS, and you should be able to see that there are 2 phrases.
-- There is an aspect of TENSION from the beginning through the 2nd beat of meas. 4. This is followed by a
    RELAXATION from the 3rd beat of meas. 4 through the cadence point of meas. 8 and 9. A similar structure
    can be found from the 3rd beat of meas. 9 through the 2nd cadence point at the end of the tune.
-- The first cadence point should be harmonized by the V chord (or V7, if Level Preparatory or Level I).
-- The second cadence point should be harmonized by the I chord.

-- The 1st cadence is an inconclusive cadence (half cadence}; the second cadence is a conclusive (authentic)
    cadence.

Continue harmonizing the rest of the tune. Keep it SIMPLE. It's OK to use the same chord consecutively, especially if the melody outlines specific chords. Keep in mind the HARMONIC RHYTHM, in this case -- one dotted half note for each measure. Notice how the first phrase cadences on a V chord and then moves to a V7 chord. This creates a stronger cadence than just cadencing on the V7 chord. Although, for Preparatory and Level I piano this will not be an option.

Notice how the V7/V chord is used at the cadence at the end of the 1st phrase (meas. 7). This is one of the most obvious uses of the V7/V chord -- right before the V chord at a HALF CADENCE.

Appendix 4: Non-Chord Tones

A NON-CHORD TONE is a note in a melody which is not part of the chord or harmony which is being used for harmonization at the point where the NON-CHORD TONE appears. Generally, there are two types of NON-CHORD TONES:

      1. Unaccented (occurs on a weak beat or a weak part of a beat)
      2. Accented (occurs on a strong beat)

The terms "accented" and "unaccented" are subjective because the "feel" of accented/unaccented depends on such factors as tempo and harmonic rhythm.

Here are some examples of NON-CHORD TONES . The numbers indicate different NON-CHORD TONES which are explained below:

1. PASSING TONE. One of the most common non-chord tones, the PASSING TONE "passes" between two adjacent chord tones. "Adjacent" means the next chord tone, either up or down. In the chord, C-E-G, "E" and "G" are adjacent but "C" and "G" are nonadjacent. So the PASSING TONE between C-E would be "D". The PASSING TONE between E-G would be F.

2. NEIGHBOR TONE. Also one of the most common-chord tones, the NEIGHBOR TONE is a diatonic step UP or DOWN from any chord tone. If the NEIGHBOR TONE is above the chord-tone then it's an "UPPER NEIGHBOR TONE." And if it's below, its called a LOWER NEIGHBOR TONE. The example above (#2) is a LOWER NEIGHBOR TONE.

3. ACCENTED PASSING TONE. If a passing tone occurs on a strong beat then it's called an ACCENTED PASSING TONE. Notice that the note before and after are chord-tones.

4. ANTICIPATION. An ANTICIPATION, "anticipates" the upcoming chord. So, this implies that at least TWO chords and 3 melody notes are involved. The 1st note is a chord tone associated with the 1st chord and the 2nd note (which is the actual ANTICIPATION) is a non-chord tone associated with the 2nd chord. In the example above (#4), the "E" is a chord-tone and is associated with the C major triad on beat 1. The "F" on beat 2 is not part of the C major triad but is a part of the F major triad on beat 3. An ANTICIPATION always occurs on a weak beat.

5. SUSPENSION. A SUSPENSION is the similar to an ANTICIPATION except that it always occurs on a STRONG beat. It must have TWO chords involved and THREE melody notes. The 1st melody note is associated with the 1st chord and occurs on a WEAK beat. The 2nd melody note is THE SAME as the 1st melody note but is associated with the second chord and occurs on a strong beat. This 2nd melody note is the actual SUSPENSION and it's a NON-CHORD TONE (not part of the 2nd chord). The 3rd melody note "resolves" to a chord tone in the 2nd chord.

6. APPOGGIATURA. An APPOGGIATURA is a type of ACCENTED non-chord tone and is very similar to a SUSPENSION: it must have TWO chords involved and THREE melody notes. Here's the difference: the 2nd melody note is DIFFERENT from the 1st melody note and it SKIPS to a non-chord tone associated with the 2nd chord and then "resolves" BY STEP in the OPPOSITE DIRECTION from the skip. If this seems complex, then just study the example. Some music theorists consider all ACCENTED non-chord tones to be APPOGGIATURAS. See "appoggiatura" in *Harvard's Dictionary of Music.*

7. ESCAPE TONE. An ESCAPE TONE occurs on a WEAK beat and consists of a step (either up or down) followed by a skip in the opposite direction to a CHORD TONE in either the same chord or a different chord.

There are other NON-CHORD TONES but they will not be discussed here. You will no doubt cover them in your theory courses.

A question that is often asked by beginning theory students is, "Good grief! Why does all this matter?" Here's a simple answer:

Music theory is the SCIENCE of music. In any scientific field, one endeavors is to CLASSIFY all possible phenomena. For example, in the field of geology, one endeavors to classify all rocks and all phenomena concerning rocks. The same is true in ornithology, entomology, astronomy, physics, etc. The study of music is no different. To UNDERSTAND music at a deep level, one has to classify and NAME all possible musical phenomena. Although this may seem tedious and unimportant to the novice, it is invaluable to the professional musician.

Weekly Assignment Schedule

Week 1: Welcome to class
Prepare to take a written quiz <u>next class period</u> on Group I and II Scales (p. 91), <u>written material only</u>. The quiz will cover as:
1. What scales are in each group?
2. What are the thumb notes of each scale in Group I?
3. What are the characteristics of the scales in each group?
4. Key signatures of any scale.

Week 2: Repertory; Scales; Cadences; Establish Keys; Harmonization; Exercises
- Scales: Group I Major scales, pp. 91-92
- Cadence #1 in all required major and minor keys, p. 48
- Establish Keys for all major keys on the white notes of the piano using the Cadence #1 progression. Some keys (E major, A major, and B major) are not written out so you will have to transpose them.
- Harmonized melodies:
  - Study the **Procedures for Harmonized Melodies**, p. 46-47
  - Take a <u>written quiz</u> in the next session (Week 3) on the **Procedures for Harmonized Melodies**, p. 46-47
  - Harmonize melodies #21, p. 55 and #12, p. 53 using the chords from Cadence #1. This is a general review of harmonizing melodies from last semester.
- Exercise #1, play up one octave, p. 104

Week 3: Repertory; Scales; Cadences; Harmonization; Improvisation; Sight Reading; Exercises
- Repertory: *Playing Soldiers*, p. 10
- Scales: Group I harmonic minor scales, pp. 91, 94
- Cadence #1 in all required major and minor keys, p. 48
- Triads: All major triads on the white keys of the piano, pp. 42-43
- Harmonized melodies: Study and practice the Accompaniment Patterns on the bottom of p. 47. Be prepare to play these on request from your instructor.
- Improvisation: Review the improvisation material on pp. 60-63. Prepare examples #1 & #2 at the bottom of p. 63. Follow the procedures listed above the chord progression examples.
- Sight Read pp. 44-45
- Exercise #1 complete, up one and down one octave, pp. 104-105

Week 4: Repertory; Scales; Cadences; Establish Keys; Harmonization; Sight Reading; Exercises
- Repertory: Your instructor may ask you to review the repertory piece from Week 3, so be prepared to play it if requested. Get started on the new repertory on page 16: ***Prologue***
- Scales: All Group I major and harmonic minor scales, pp. 91 - 94
- Cadence #2 in C Major, p. 49
- Establish Keys for all major keys on the white notes of the piano using the Cadence #1 progression.
- Harmonized melodies: Harmonize melody #31, p. 47 using block chords from Cadence #2 (and an accompaniment pattern if your instructor request it).
- Sight Read p. 46
- Exercise #1 complete, up one and down octave; Exercise #2, play up one octave, pp. 104-106

Week 5: Repertory; Scales; Cadences; Improvisation; Transposition; Sight Reading; Exercises
- Repertory: *Prologue*, p. 16
- Scales: Group II scales, C Major, hands separate and together, up and down ONE octave, pp. 92, 95
- Cadence #2 in all required major keys, p. 49
- Improvisation: Review the improvisation material on pp. 60-63. Prepare example #1 at the bottom of p. 66. Follow the procedures listed above the chord progression examples.
- Transposition: Transpose #1, p. 68 hands separately. Transpose the example up and down a half step and a whole step.
- Sight Read pp. 44--46
- Exercises: #1 & 2 complete; pp. 104-107

Week 6: Repertory; Scales; Cadences; Triads; Establish Keys; Sight Reading; Exercises
- Repertory: Your instructor may ask you to review the repertory piece from Week 5, so be prepared to play it if requested. Get started on the new repertory on page 26: ***Two Etudes, No. 1***
- Scales: Group II scales, C Major, hands separate and together, up and down TWO octave, pp. 92, 95
- Cadences: Cadence #2 in all required major keys, p. 49
- Triads: All major triads on the white keys of the piano, pp. 42-43
- Establish Keys for all minor keys on the white notes of the piano using the Cadence #1 progression.
- Sight Read p. 72
- Exercises: #1 & 2 complete; pp. 104-107

Week 7: Repertory; Scales; Cadences; Harmonization; Improvisation; Sight Reading; Exercises
- Repertory: *Two Études, No. 1*, p. 26
- Scales: All Group II Major scales, 2 octaves up and down, pp. 92, 95
- Cadences: Cadence #2 in all required minor keys, p. 49
- Harmonized melodies: Harmonize melody #32, p. 57 using block chords from Cadence #2 (and an accompaniment pattern if your instructor request it).
- Improvisation: Review the improvisation material on pp. 60-63. Prepare example #2 at the bottom of p. 66. Follow the procedures listed above the chord progression examples.
- Sight Read p. 73
- Exercises: #1 & 2 complete; pp. 104-107

Week 8: Repertory; Scales; Cadences; Triads; Establish Keys; Harmonization; Transposition; Sight Reading; Exercises
- Repertory: Your instructor may ask you to review the repertory piece from Week 7, so be prepared to play it if requested. Get started on the new repertory on page 30: ***Country Dance***
- Scales: Scales: All Group II natural minor scales, 2 octaves up and down, pp. 92, 96
- Cadences: Cadence #2 in all required minor keys, p. 49
- Triads: All minor triads on the white keys of the piano, pp. 42-43
- Establish Keys for all minor keys on the white notes of the piano using the Cadence #1 progression.
- Review Rules for Harmonization, p. 44 - 45
- Transposition: Transpose #6, p. 69 hands separately. Transpose the example up and down a half step and a whole step.
- Sight Read p. 74
- Exercises: #1 & 2 complete; Exercise #3 up one octave; pp. 104-108

Week 9: Repertory; Scales; Cadences; Improvisation; Sight Reading; Exercises
- Repertory: *Country Dance*, p. 30
- Scales: All Group II harmonic minor scales, 2 octaves up and down, pp. 92, 97
- Cadences: Cadence #2 in all required major and minor keys, pp. 48-49
- Improvisation: Review the improvisation material on pp. 60-63. Prepare example #3 at the bottom of p. 66. Follow the procedures listed above the chord progression examples.
- Sight Read p. 75
- Exercise #1, 2, & 3 complete, pp. 104-109

Week 10: Repertory; Scales; Cadences; Establish Keys; Harmonization; Sight Reading; Exercises
- Repertory: Your instructor may ask you to review the repertory piece from Week 9, so be prepared to play it if requested. There will not be any new repertory pieces assigned. However, you should start considering which repertory you will choose for your final exam on Week 15. This can be a new repertory piece approved by your instructor, or it can be any of the repertory studied after Week 4. Ask your instructor for details.
- Scales: All Group II melodic minor scales, 2 octaves up and down, pp. 92, 98
- Cadences: Cadence #2 in all required major and minor keys, pp. 48-49
- Establish Keys for all major and minor keys on the white notes of the piano using the Cadence #1 progression.
- Harmonized melodies: Harmonize melody #34, p. 58 using block chords from Cadence #2 (and an accompaniment pattern if your instructor request it).
- Sight Read p. 54, each part separately
- Exercise #1, 2, & 3 complete, pp. 104-109

Week 11: Repertory; Scales; Cadences; Triads; Improvisation; Transposition; Sight Reading; Exercises
- Repertory: You will be required to play a repertory piece from memory at the end of the semester as part of your final exam. In consultation with your instructor you may choose any repertory from the book and begin preparing it from memory over the next several weeks. It may be a new piece, or if your instructor recommends it, it may be one of the pieces you have already worked on for this semester. Begin working on your selection and be prepared to play all or part of it for a grade next week.
- *What Wondrous Love...,* p. 26
- Scales: Review all Group II Scales, pp. 92-98
- Cadences: Cadence #2 in all required major and minor keys, pp. 48-49
- Improvisation: Review the improvisation material on pp. 60-63. Prepare example #4 at the bottom of p. 66. Follow the procedures listed above the chord progression examples.
- Transposition: Transpose #10, p. 70 hands separately. Transpose the example up and down a half step and a whole step.
- Triads: All minor triads on the white keys of the piano, pp. 42-43
- Sight Read p. 55, each part separately
- Exercise #1, 2, & 3 complete, pp. 104-109

Week 12: Repertory; Scales; Triads; Cadences; Improvisation; Establish Keys; Sight Reading; Exercises
- Repertory: You will be required to play a repertory piece from memory at the end of the semester as part of your final exam. In consultation with your instructor you may choose any repertory from the book and begin preparing it from memory over the next several weeks. It may be a new piece, or if your instructor recommends it, it may be one of the pieces you have already worked on for this semester. Begin working on your selection and be prepared to play all or part of it for a grade.
- Scales: All Group I & II Scales, pp. 91-98
- Cadences: Cadence #2 in all required major and minor keys, pp. 48-49
- Establish Keys for all major and minor keys on the white notes of the piano using the Cadence #1 progression.
- Triads: All major and minor root position triads on the white keys of the piano, p. 42-45
- Improvisation: Do Improvisation Example #4, p. 61 (top of the page)
- Sight Read pp. 48-49
- Exercise #1, 2, & 3 complete, pp. 104-109

Please READ THIS: A memorized repertory piece will be required for your final exam. Ask your instructor for details.

Week 13: Repertory; Scales; Triads; Cadences; Harmonized melody; Establish Keys; Sight Reading; Exercises
- Repertory: Continue working on your selected repertory piece which you will play from memory at the end of of the semester. Be prepared to play all or part of it for a grade.
  • This piece (*Capriccio*) will be due for a grade on Week 15.
  • You will have to MEMORIZE this piece (*Capriccio*) and play it as part of a FINAL EXAM.*
- Scales: All Group I & II Scales, pp. 91-98
- Triads: All Triads, p. 42-45
- Cadences: Cadence #2 in all required major and minor keys, pp. 48-49
- Harmonized melodies: Harmonize melody #12, p. 53 using block chords from Cadence #2 (and an accompaniment pattern if your instructor request it). It is possible to use a V7/7 chord at the half cadence event though it may sound somewhat dissonant. This give a kind of "sharp-9" sound to the accompaniment which is characteristic of jazz or some contemporary classical music.
- Establish Keys for all major and minor keys on the white notes of the piano using the Cadence #1 progression.
- Triads: All major and minor root position triads on the white keys of the piano, p. 32-33
- Sight Read pp. 8-9
- Exercise #1, 2, & 3 complete, pp. 104-109

Week 14: Repertory; Scales; Triads; Cadences; Establish Keys; Harmonization; Improvisation; Harmonization; Sight Reading; Exercises
- Repertory: Continue working on your selected repertory piece which you will play from memory at the end of

of the semester. Be prepared to play all or part of it for a grade.
- Scales: All Group I & II Scales, pp. 91-98
- Triads: All Triads, p. 42-45
- Cadences: Cadence #2 in all required major and minor keys, pp. 48-49
- Establish Keys for all major and minor keys on the white notes of the piano using the Cadence #1 progression.
- Triads: All major and minor root position triads on the white keys of the piano, p. 32-33
- Harmonize melody #36 on p. 58 using the chords from Cadence #2.
- Transposition: Transpose #12, p. 71 hands separately. Transpose the example up and down a half step and a whole step.
- Sight Read pp. 10-11
- Exercise #1, 2, & 3 complete, pp. 104-109

Week 15: Repertory; Scales; Triads; Cadences; Establish Keys; Harmonization; Improvisation; Transposition; Sight Reading; Exercises;
- Repertory: Your selected repertory is due this week from MEMORY.
- In addition to your memorized repertory, have all the following material prepared. Your instructor may hear any of it for this week's assignment:
  • Scales: All Group I & II Scales, pp. 91-98
  • Triads: All major and minor root position triads on the white keys of the piano, p. 42-45
  • All Cadences studied this semester: Cadence #1 & 2 in all required major and minor keys, pp. 48-49
  • Establish Keys for all major and minor keys on the white notes
  • Harmonize melody #33 on p. 57 using the chords from Cadence #2.
  • Transposition: Transpose #9, p. 70 hands separately. Transpose the example up and down a half step and a whole step.
  • Improvisation: Be able to do any of the Improvisation examples at the bottom of p. 61. Follow the procedures listed above the chord progression examples.
  • Be prepared to Sight Read any example given to you by your instructor.
  • Exercise #1, 2, & 3 complete, pp. 104-109

*A Final Exam may be arranged by the Instructor.

Class Notes

Level Two Assignments

WK	Scales	Repertory	Cadences	Estab. a Key	Improv.	Harm. Mel.	*Transp.	Triads.	SIGHT READING	Exercises
1	Written quiz Scale Groups 1 & 2 -- see p. 91									
2	Gr. 1 Majors		#1, p. 48 Maj & Min keys	Maj keys White notes		#21, p. 55 #12, p. 53			p. 68	#1, p. 104
3	Gr. 1 Minors	p. 10 *Playing Soldiers*	#1, p. 48 Maj & Min key		#1, p. 63 #2, p. 63			All Major	p. 69	#1, p. 104
4	All Gr. 1		#2, p. 49 C major	Maj keys White notes		#31, p. 57			p. 70	#1 & 2 pp. 104- - 107
5	Gr. 2 C Maj 1 octave	p. 16 *Prologue*	#2, p. 49 Maj keys		#1, p. 66		#1 p. 68		p. 71	#1 & 2 pp. 104- - 107
6	Gr. 2 C Maj 2 octaves		#2, p. 49 Maj keys	Min keys White notes				All Major	p. 72	#1 & 2 pp. 104- - 107
7	Gr. 2 Majors	p. 28 *Two Études, No. 1*	#2, p. 49 Min keys		#2, p. 66	#32, p. 57			p. 73	#1 & 2 pp. 104- - 107
8	Gr. 2 Nat min		#2, p. 49 Min keys	Min keys White notes			#6 p. 69	All Minor	p. 74	#1, 2. 3 pp. 104-109
9	Gr. 2 Har min	p. 30 *Country Dance*	#2, p. 49		#3, p. 66				p. 75	#1, 2. 3 pp. 104-109
10	Gr. 2 Mel min		#2, p. 49	All keys White notes		#34, p. 58		All Minor	p. 76	#1, 2. 3 pp. 104-109
11	All Gr. 2		#2, p. 49	All keys White notes	#4, p. 66		#10 p. 70		p. 77	#1, 2. 3 pp. 104-109
12	All Scales to date	Rep. piece of choice**	#2, p. 49	All keys White notes				All Maj/Min	pp. 68-72	#1, 2. 3 pp. 104-109
13	All Scales to date	Your selection**	#2, p. 49	All keys White notes		#12, p. 53		All Maj/Min	pp. 73-77	#1, 2. 3 pp. 104-109
14	All Scales to date	Your selection**	#2, p. 49	All keys White notes		#36, p. 58	#12 p. 71	All Maj/Min	pp. 68-77	#1, 2. 3 pp. 104-109
15	All Scales to date	Your selection memorized**	#2, p. 49	All keys White notes	any p. 66	#33, p. 57	#9 p. 70	All Maj/Min	pp. 68-88	#1, 2. 3 pp. 104-109

All scales,, cadences, triads, and exercises should be performed from memory when playing for a grade. Failure to do so will result in a lowered grade.

* Regarding the TRANSPOSITION assignments, students are only required to play one part at a time; however, both parts should be prepared. In examples where both hands are the same an octave apart, play both hands together and not separately. Prepare each example UP a whole step, DOWN a whole step, UP a half step, DOWN a half.

** Your "piece of choice" beginning in week 12 can be a new piece or any piece after Week 4. You will memorize this piece and play it from memory on Week 15.